TEACHING CONCEPTS

An Instructional
Design Guide

TEACHING CONCEPTS:
AN INSTRUCTIONAL DESIGN GUIDE

M. David Merrill
Brigham Young University

Robert D. Tennyson
University of Minnesota

EDUCATIONAL TECHNOLOGY PUBLICATIONS
ENGLEWOOD CLIFFS, NEW JERSEY 07632

Library of Congress Cataloging in Publication Data

Merrill, M   David
  Teaching concepts.

  Bibliography: p.
  Includes index.
  1. Teaching. 2. Behavior modification. I. Tenny-
son, Robert D., joint author. II. Title.
LB1025.2.M447   371.1'02   76-28182
ISBN 0-87778-093-5

Printed in the United States of America.

Library of Congress Catalog Card Number:
76-28182.

International Standard Book Number:
0-87778-093-5.

First Printing: January, 1977.
Second Printing: April, 1981.
Third Printing, January, 1987.

A NOTE TO THE READER

The procedures outlined in this book may appear to be extremely laborious compared to procedures you are now using to prepare instructional materials. However, after you have prepared several lessons using the recommended procedures you will find that your planning efficiency has actually increased. In addition, your students will find your lessons more enjoyable and much easier to understand.

PREFACE

During the past decade there has been considerable research on strategies for teaching "classroom like" concepts. The concepts taught and the strategies investigated by this effort differ considerably from the type of concepts which have often been investigated by experimental psychologists. While there is much work yet to be done, there has evolved from this research a set of very specific, empirically validated procedures for teaching concepts. If followed, these procedures provide far more adequate concept instruction than that typically seen in classrooms or mediated instructional materials. The following paragraphs briefly summarize these procedures.

Procedures for
Teaching Concepts
1. *Present a definition.*
   A "definition" is a statement identifying each of the critical attributes and indicating how these attributes are combined.

2. *Provide an expository presentation of a set of matched example/nonexample pairs in which subsequent examples are divergent from the preceding examples and which range in difficulty from easy to hard.*
   An "expository presentation" is one in which a student is told that each given instance is an example or is not an example. A "matched example/nonexample pair" is a situation in which the

variable attributes of the example and the matched nonexample are as similar as possible. "Divergent" indicates that the variable attributes of subsequent examples are as different as possible from the variable attributes of the preceding examples. "Difficulty" is the ease with which members of a specified student population, given only a definition, are able to correctly classify a given instance as either an example or a nonexample.

It has been demonstrated that failure to meet one or more of these conditions can result in particular classification errors. Using all easy examples will produce *undergeneralization*. Eliminating nonexamples, or failing to match nonexamples to examples, will produce *overgeneralization*. Using convergent examples, that is, examples in which the variable attributes are similar, will produce a *misconception*.

3. *Provide attribute isolation help for each example and nonexample in the expository presentation.*

"Attribute isolation" is achieved through the use of attention-focusing devices such as color, exploded drawings, arrows, heavy type, etc., which enable the student to isolate more easily the critical attributes from the variable attributes in the instance under consideration.

4. *Provide an inquisitory practice presentation of newly encountered examples and nonexamples arranged in random sequence accompanied by helped feedback.*

An "inquisitory practice" presentation is one which displays an instance, either an example or a nonexample, and asks the student to indicate whether it is a member of the class under consideration. "Newly encountered" indicates that the instances used in practice are different from those used during the presentation. "Helped feedback" is information, provided for each student after he/she responds, which includes the correct answer and attribute isolation help which focuses attention on the critical attributes or potentially confusing variable attributes of the instance under consideration. A "random sequence" in practice provides for student classification experience without the contextual cues which result from carefully matched example/non-example pairs and divergent subsequent examples.

5. *Correct classification is tested by means of an inquisitory test presentation consisting of a sufficient number and variety of randomly sequenced, newly encountered instances to allow reliable and valid inference about subsequent classification behavior of yet to be encountered instances of the concept being taught.*

A "sufficient number" is a number large enough to provide some evidence for an estimate of reliability. "Variety" indicates that the examples selected should include several of the possible variable attribute configurations in which examples of the concept can occur. In other words, the examples and nonexamples selected for the test should be divergent but should be randomly sequenced so that this divergence is not emphasized.

Purpose

The purpose of this book is to teach, in detail, how to design and develop instructional materials using the above procedures. Each of the prescriptions to be taught has been tested and validated in carefully controlled experimental research studies. These prescriptions will be discussed in depth in the chapters which follow.

Teaching Concepts is a very practical book. It was designed to assist teachers, instructional developers, curriculum planners, textbook authors, and others who are concerned with effective instructional strategies to teach concepts more adequately. The writing style is non-academic; there is little attempt to reference sources, credit authors with similar views, or present alternative viewpoints. The emphasis is on "how to" rather than "why." The approach is instructional rather than comprehensive. The procedures used to design this book are the same as those advocated in the book. The book presents an integrated set of procedures rather than a review of alternative procedures. It is rich in illustrative materials and in instructional devices which may facilitate learning.

This is an unusual book in at least two ways. First, it is concerned with only one kind of lesson, a lesson designed to teach a concept or a set of coordinate concepts. Second, it is an *instructional design guide* which gives you the directions for designing concept lessons. If you follow the directions carefully, you will be able to design concept lessons that are probably better than you have ever previously taught.

What Is Instructional Design?

Instructional design is a fancy phrase which means selecting and arranging instructional materials in a way which helps students learn more efficiently and effectively than they could from a natural situation. It also means selecting and arranging special materials which allow you as a teacher, or the students as learners, to find out whether they have learned what you intended.

How Should This Book Be Used?

First, you should read the whole book quickly. Second, you should study each section as you carry out the instructional design step being discussed. You should not read the book only once and then try to design concept lessons, without looking at it again. This book is like a recipe. After you have made a recipe several times, you can do it without the directions; but at first you will be more successful if you follow the directions step-by-step. After you have designed a number of different concept lessons, you will be able to use ideas presented without referring to the guide; at first, however, your lessons will be better if you *follow the directions carefully.*

Let Us Hear From You

We sincerely hope that you will experiment with these designs and that once you have mastered the steps explained in this guide you will try modifications of the procedures and new procedures. If your approaches are more effective than the techniques described here, please share them with us.

The authors of this book are involved in a continuing program of systematic research on the teaching of concepts. The Appendix of this volume provides a brief synopsis of some of the research which has been published. We invite inquiries from readers concerning our current activities. The revision of this guide commenced as soon as the manuscript went to press. We want to be sure that subsequent editions reflect the most current knowledge about teaching concepts. If you or your colleagues are engaged in related research we would appreciate your sharing reports of this activity with the authors.

MDM RDT
June, 1976

TABLE OF CONTENTS

TEACHING CONCEPTS

An Instructional
Design Guide

CHAPTER 1

BEFORE YOU BEGIN

**WHAT IS
A CONCEPT?**
A concept is a set of specific objects, symbols, or events which are grouped together on the basis of shared characteristics and which can be referenced by a particular name or symbol.

Most of the words in any given language refer to classes or categories of symbols, objects, or events rather than to particular instances of these categories. Usually it is necessary to use modifying words to make one of these general class words refer to a particular instance.

> **Example:** The word "cat" refers to a set of objects which share particular characteristics such that one can learn to distinguish cats from dogs, rabbits, rats, or anything else. Any given cat represents a member of the general set, cat. In order to refer to a specific cat, one must use modifying words to make the general word specific. Thus *"my* cat," "that cat by *the fence*," "the *yellow* cat *by the fireplace*" illustrate the use of modifying words to make the general category "cat" specific to a particular instance.

Instances of object concepts exist in time and space and can easily be represented by drawings, photographs, models, or the object itself.

Example: Merely scanning the pages of the dictionary demonstrates that there are many object concept words, such as: aardvark, abacus, abalone, . . . baboon, baby, ballerina, . . .

Nonexamples: There are fewer words that refer to a particular object, such as Aarhus (a seaport in Eastern Jutland, Denmark). Aaron (in the Bible, the older brother of Moses), . . . Baal (among ancient peoples a sun god), Babel (a city in Shinar, Biblical). These words are not concept labels but identities.* Note that most of these identifies are proper names.

Many of the concepts which must be taught are symbol concepts. Symbol concepts consist of particular kinds of words, numbers, marks, and numerous other items that represent or describe objects, events, or their relationships either real or imagined.

Examples: From the study of language we have symbol concepts, such as noun, verb, subject, predicate, paragraph, topic sentence. From mathematics we have symbol concepts, such as unknown, equation, whole number, fraction, decimal, integer, numerator, denominator.

Event concepts are interactions of objects, either living or inorganic, in a particular way and in a particular period of time. Event concepts are often the most difficult to grasp because it is difficult to adequately capture and represent a given instance of an event for presentation in an instructional situation.

Examples: Some event concept names include: acceleration, banishment, censorship, diagnosis, football game, riot, marriage, birthday party, mitosis, photosynthesis, digestion, reinforcement, punishment, growth.

---

*Since a concept has been defined as a set, and since a set can have as few as one member, identities are concepts. To avoid confusion, when a concept set contains only a single member or when all of the members of a set are essentially identical, we have eliminated them from consideration as a concept lesson.

The word concept sometimes refers to an idea as held in the mind of a person; however, in this guide we will assume that a set of instances grouped by one person, a group, or society at large can be described and identified independently of the idea in the mind by a particular student. The primary purpose of instruction is to assist one person, the student, to group together the same instances that another person, the teacher, groups together by a concept name or symbol. A student is said to have learned a concept when he/she classifies the individual instances of the set the same way that the instructor classifies them.

In a very real sense all concepts are arbitrary, because people impose classes on the world; classes do not exist in some ultimate sense independently of people. Hence, a given concept may be unique with a single person. When he/she tries to communicate his/her classification to another person, he/she becomes the teacher, and the person to whom he/she is trying to communicate becomes the student. In school settings teachers usually try to communicate concept classes which are agreed to by some larger groups of people, like all physicists, botanists, English teachers, or members of a particular social group. In this case there are two questions to deal with: Does the teacher validly represent the concept as held by the group he/she represents? Is he/she adequately presenting the concept to the student? This guide is concerned primarily with the second process rather than the first.

CLASSIFICATION BEHAVIOR *A student has learned a concept when he/she can correctly identify the class membership of a specific symbol, object, or event.*

Classification behavior occurs when, given a specific symbol, object, or event, the student can name or point to the general word that refers to a class to which the specific instance belongs;

or, when given the general name of the class and shown representations of specific instances of this and other classes, the student will be able to identify those symbols, objects, or events which are members of the class and those symbols, objects, or events which are not members of the class.

Examples: The following test questions each require classification behavior.	**Nonexamples:** * The following test questions involve the same concepts as those in the left hand column but do not involve classification behavior.
Below are pictures of clouds. Under each picture write the word cirrus, cumulus, or nimbus to indicate the type of clouds pictured.	Match the name of the cloud with its description by writing the description's number after the name:

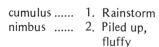

Name   Description

cumulus ......   1. Rainstorm
nimbus ......   2. Piled up,
                    fluffy
cirrus   ......   3. Curly,
                    whispy

Underline the single word modifiers in each of the following sentences and draw an arrow to the head word which they modify:

1. The old church stood on a high hill.

A word which clarifies the meaning of another word is called a ....

---

*Later in this book we will teach you how to use matched example/nonexample pairs. Note that this is an example of the procedure we will teach you to use.

2.   The young man walked quickly through the crowd.

Two chemical processes are iillustrated below. What is each called?

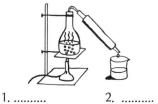

1. ....   2. ....

Condensation is:

a.   A physical change from gas to liquid.
b.   A physical change from liquid to gas.
c.   A chemical change from gas to liquid.
d.   A chemical change from liquid to gas.

GENERALIZATION AND DISCRIMINATION

There are two psychological processes involved in classification behavior: generalization and discrimination.

GENERALIZATION occurs when a learner exhibits a particular response in one stimulus situation which he acquired in a similar stimulus situation.

DISCRIMINATION occurs when a learner exhibits a particular response in one stimulus situation but a different response in a similar stimulus situation.

All learners have a natural tendency to generalize. Responses which are reinforced in one situation are tried in similar situations. It is this process (combined with discrimination) which enables a learner to adapt to new circumstances. If we did not generalize, an appropriate response would have to be learned in every new situation; this would greatly increase the amount of learning necessary, and inhibit a learner's ability to adapt to his/her environment.

Discrimination, the opposite process, allows the learner to stop generalizing and to make fine distinctions between very similar situations. Discrimination allows the learner to respond differently to changes in stimuli, to communicate precisely, and to deal with the complexity of his/her environment. Discrimination must be promoted by appropriate feedback to the learner concerning his responses.

Examples of generalization:

In the learning laboratory, generalization has been demonstrated and studied with many different organisms. If a pigeon learns to peck a colored disk in order to obtain food, it will continue to peck when the color of the disk is changed gradually. If the change is too great, however, the pigeon will cease pecking.

In a classical conditioning experiment, if a dog comes to salivate at the sound of a bell, he will also salivate if the tone of the bell is changed and eventually he will salivate to a buzzer or whistle.

Examples of discrimination:*

In the learning laboratory, a pigeon can learn to peck at a red disk of a particular wave length but not to peck when the wave length is changed only slightly. This fine discrimination must be brought about gradually by providing food when the disk is pecked when red, but not when it is orange and then gradually changing the orange until it is almost identical to the red.

Rats can learn to press a bar to get food when a light is on and to not press the bar when the light is off. The discrimination is promoted by providing food in one situation but not in the other.

---

*Later in this book we will discuss teaching two or more coordinate concepts simultaneously. In this situation the examples of one concept become the nonexamples of the other. Note here that examples of *generalization* are nonexamples of *discrimination,* while examples of *discrimination* are nonexamples of *generalization.* We have still used matched example/nonexample pairs but the nonexample depends on which of the two concepts you are considering at the moment.

When a child first learns the word "daddy" he will frequently apply the name to all adult male persons. When he applies the name to a new male person, he is generalizing. If a man is very different from his father, e.g., much larger or bearded, then the child may not generalize.

If corrected by his parents, a child who calls every male "daddy" will come to discriminate his father from other males and to apply the word "man" to those males who are not his father. Eventually he will learn finer discriminations such as "mailman" and "milkman." Such discriminations are learned as a result of corrective feedback from parents and peers.

When learning to talk in sentences and to apply new grammatical patterns, children often generalize inappropriately. Having learned to add an "ed" sound to express an occurance in the past a child will generalize the rule to all verbs and tries combinations like "he runned" or "she swimmed." Both correct and incorrect applications of such grammatical rules represent generalization.

When a child inappropriately generalizes a grammatical rule and is corrected, he comes to discriminate those situations where "ed" changes a verb to past tense and those situations where some other change is required, such as "ran" or "swam."

When generalization and discrimination are applied to classes of objects, symbols, or events it is called classification behavior. A student has acquired a concept when he/she can correctly generalize the application of the class name to all members of the class, while correctly discriminating among members which belong to other classes. In short, classification behavior is generalization within a class and simultaneous discrimination among classes.

Example: The following diagram illustrates generalization within and discrimination between classes.

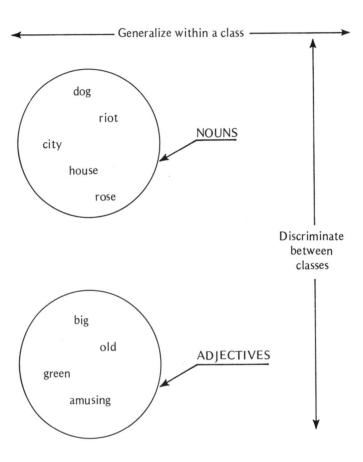

The first circle encloses words representing the set of all nouns. The second circle encloses words representing the set of all adjectives. When a learner understands the concept noun, he/she should be able to generalize the response noun to any specific noun, even if he/she has never been told that the new word is a noun. At the same time, shown an adjective, he/she should not generalize, but should be able to discriminate nouns from adjectives.

POTENTIALLY   *ASSOCIATION   BEHAVIOR   occurs*
CONFUSING   *when a student is asked to associate two*
BEHAVIORS   *specific symbols, objects, or events by*
                           being able to name one when shown the
                           other.

                           RULE-USING BEHAVIOR occurs when
                           a student is asked to combine objects,
                           symbols, or events from two or more
                           classes by means of some operation to
                           form an object symbol or event in a
                           resulting concept class.

                           DO NOT CONFUSE THESE BEHAV-
                           IORS WITH CLASSIFICATION BE-
                           HAVIOR.

There are many association tasks (often called memorization tasks) which do not involve classification behavior. This guide is not intended to be a recipe for teaching these tasks.

Examples: Association behavior occurs when a student is able to point out and name the stellar constellations. This behavior requires the student to associate one set of objects, the stars, with another set of corresponding symbols, the constellation names.

Association behavior occurs when a student can name the notes of the treble staff in music. This behavior requires the student to associate one set of symbols, the notes, with a corresponding set of symbols, the letter names.

Some types of learned behavior require more than single classification. In these behaviors the student must combine instances (the objects, symbols, or events) from two or more concepts to produce an instance of a new concept. Rule using behavior may involve classification as one or more of the steps in the process, but it also involves additional behaviors.

> **Example**: Solving a linear equation involves several steps. The student must first recognize the unknown. This is classification behavior. He/she must then add, subtract, multiply, or divide both sides of the equation by equal amounts until he/she has isolated the unknown. Then he/she must use these arithmetic operations to find the value of the unknown. These operations require more than classification.

Rule using may involve classification behavior as part of the process but it also requires operation using. This guide will be helpful in teaching the classification part of rule using but will not provide guidance for teaching operation using.

SUMMARY	*BEFORE YOU BEGIN*
WHAT IS A CONCEPT?	*1.* *A concept is a set of specific objects, symbols, or events which are grouped together on the basis of shared characteristics and which can be referenced by a particular name or symbol.*
	A student has learned a concept when he can correctly identify the class membership of a specific symbol, object, or event.
WHAT IS CLASSIFICATION BEHAVIOR?	*2.* *There are two psychological processes involved in classification behavior: generalization and discrimination.*

Generalization occurs when a learner exhibits a particular response in one stimulus situation which he/she acquired in a similar stimulus situation.

Discrimination occurs when a learner exhibits a particular response in one stimulus situation but a different response in a similar stimulus situation.

3. *DON'T CONFUSE ASSOCIATION BEHAVIOR AND RULE-USING BEHAVIOR WITH CLASSIFICATION BEHAVIOR. Association behavior occurs when a student is asked to associate two specific symbols, objects, or events by being able to name one when shown the other. Rule using behavior occurs when a student is asked to combine objects, symbols, or events from two or more classes by means of some operation to form an object, symbol, or event in a resulting concept class.*

CHAPTER 2

STEP 1:
DECIDE IF A CONCEPT
LESSON IS NEEDED

YOU
DECIDE

Content and behavior are somewhat independent. A student can be taught to memorize, classify, use a rule, or find a rule for almost any topic.

The behavior required by the student depends on the conditions under which the student is allowed or required to make a particular response in regard to a particular kind of content material. Consequently, a given text book, curriculum guide, or other content source does not necessarily determine whether a concept lesson is required.

Example: Consider the topic "linear equation." The following questions (conditions) each require a different level of behavior with respect to this topic.

Question 1. Define a linear equation.

Question 1 requires the student to recall a definition. This is memorization behavior.

Question 2. Which of the following is a linear equation?

a. $x^2 = 7x + 13$
b. $X + 10X = 43$
c. $A^2 + B^2 = 0$
d. $14 + 17 = ?$

Question 2 requires the student to determine whether each instance is a linear equation (classification behavior). If the student had already been shown these same instances and told which were linear equations, then the behavior could be memorization. The change in conditions (from newly encountered to previously encountered examples) changes the behavior.

Question 3. In the following linear equation find the value of Y.

$$Y = 3Y - 12 + 2Y$$

Question 3 requires the student to use a set of operations to find an answer (rule using behavior).

Question 4. Find an equation for determining the area of a trapezoid.

Question 4 requires the student to invent or determine a rule which can be used to solve a particular class of problems (rule finding behavior). The rule to be found happens to be a linear equation.

The conditions of instruction and evaluation determine the type of behavior required of the student. The following guidelines may help you decide whether a concept lesson might be appropriate.

NEW   *Whenever you want the learner to "un-*
TERMS   *derstand," "know how to use," or*
                  "know the meaning of" a <u>new</u> <u>term</u> then
                  a classification lesson is in order.

From your own experience you can probably remember that it is all the new words that make a course in a new area difficult. Most of these new words stand for classes of objects or events. To make satisfactory progress in this new area it is necessary that you know that specific objects, events, or symbols are members of each of the categories represented by the new terms. *In short, as an instructor you should design a concept lesson for each important new word that you introduce to your students.*

Examples: Below are a few of the new terms often encountered by students in some selected areas of study.

ART

positive and negative shapes
complementary colors
balanced composition

BIOLOGY

mitosis
cell
nucleus

CHEMISTRY

composition, decomposition
solution
compound
element

PHYSICS

translucent, transparent, opaque
mass, force, acceleration

ENGLISH

adverb, adjective, noun,
trochaic meter, iambic meter,
simile, metaphor,
plot, climax

SOCIAL STUDIES

conservative, liberal,
isolationism, imperialism,
propaganda

DEFINITIONS

Whenever lesson material calls for a definition a concept lesson is probably needed.

Examples: The following statements indicate potential concept lessons.

The student, should *be familiar* with the following: conditioned response, unconditioned response, conditioned stimulus, unconditioned stimulus. The student should know the meaning of positive and negative reinforcement.

The student should *be able to define* the following phenomena: antecedent stream, anticline, back swamp, bedding plane, columnar jointing.

Occasionally lesson material suggests that a student define terms which refer to specific events, symbols, or objects. You will need to examine each case individually to be sure that what the student is required to define is a class word rather than a specific instance of some class.

Example: If an item suggested that the student define the "Attack on Pearl Harbor" you should recognize that this does not represent a class of objects or events, but rather a specific event. The word define in this context is used incorrectly to mean describe, remember, state the significance of, etc. All of these terms suggest primarily memorization behavior and do not require concept lessons. It should be recognized, however, that the "Attack on Pearl Harbor" may be an example of some broader concept, such as surprise attacks.

Often the number of new terms which can be defined in a given subject area is very large. If all of these words are taught as concepts, the time required for instruction may be impractical. This means that you must judge and select only those terms that are critical to the subject matter, rather than trying to teach them all. Don't err in the other direction, however, and fool yourself into thinking that by requiring only a definition you can cover more material.

In fact, you are asking the student to perform at a lower level of behavior (memorization) and you will end up teaching less.

RULE
USING
If the content you are teaching involves rule-using behavior, examine each rule and prepare a concept lesson for the important concepts involved.

As indicated in an earlier section, rule using usually involves more than classification behavior. However, every rule consists of a series of concepts. If a student is to be able to use a rule effectively, then he/she must understand each of the concepts involved. This means that he/she should be able to identify specific instances of objects, events, or symbols comprising each of the concepts involved in the rule. Therefore, you should carefully examine each rule to identify any new concepts the student may not understand. Each concept should be taught using a concept lesson.

Examples: Consider the following rule statements, keeping in mind that if students are to be able to apply the rule correctly they must be able to classify instances of the component concepts as indicated.

Rule (Newton's Third Law of Motion): For every action there is an equal but opposite reaction.

The component concepts are action, opposite, equal, and reaction.

Sometimes it is reasonable to assume that the students already have acquired some or all of the component concepts. In Newton's Law the word action is used in a technical sense. Ability to classify instances according to this technical definition is critical if the student is to be able to use the rule properly.

Rule: The area of a triangle is one-half the base times the altitude. Area units are the square of the units used to measure the base and altitude.

The component concepts are base, altitude, one-half, and times.

To use this rule a student must be able to identify the base and altitude as well as to use the mathematics concepts involved. If the student thinks one of the sides is the altitude, he will be unable to use the rule.

LIST
THE
STEPS

Whenever the content suggests a series of steps, examine each step and decide whether it justifies a separate concept lesson.

When the lesson material calls for the student to list the steps leading to some event or involved in some occurrence, the individual steps may be concepts and should be taught using appropriate concept lessons.

Example: Consider the following objective from social studies.

Objective: List the events leading up to the "Boston Tea Party."

The Colonists felt that it was unlawful to have "taxation without representation." "Taxation without representation" is a concept. Other examples could be cited or invented to help students understand this idea. Merely reciting the steps leading up to the event, without understanding the concept, is not good instruction. Hence a concept lesson is suggested.

Steps in a process which involve a class of objects or events should also be taught using appropriate concept lessons.

Example: A series of steps in using a microscope may call for the student to "prepare a 'wet mount' using a drop of pond water." The student's ability to carry out this step will be facilitated if he is given a short concept lesson in which he learns to distinguish "wet mount" slides from "dry mount" slides.

IDENTIFY
PARTS

If the lesson material calls for the learner to identify parts, examine the task and decide if some of the parts to be identified should be taught as concepts.

Most often, material that requires the student to identify parts involves specific associations and should be taught as an association task. However, the parts to be identified may represent more general classes; then a concept lesson is desirable.

Example: Consider the following example from zoology.

Objective: From a dissected preserved organism identify each of the following: esophagus, trachea, bronchi, diaphragm, lungs, pericardial sac, and heart.

This task could be learned as a specific association using any of the following procedures: show pictures, have student point out specific parts, use single organism (e.g., cat) both for teaching and testing. However, since learning to identify anatomical objects (e.g., the set of trachea, etc.) in various organisms is the implied goal, each anatomical part on the list could be more adequately taught as a concept lesson using the procedures described in this guide. Identifying the trachea in different organisms is concept classification; finding the trachea in a single organism is an association.

SUMMARY **STEP 1:**	*DECIDE IF A CONCEPT* *LESSON IS NEEDED*

NEW TERMS	*1. Does the material involve new terms?*
	     Yes! Prepare a concept lesson for each important new term or related set of new terms.
	
	     Does the material require the student to define new words?
	     Yes! Prepare a concept lesson for each important new word or related set of new words.

RULE USING

2. *Does the content involve rule using?*
   Yes! Prepare a concept lesson for each component concept in the rule.

LIST
THE
STEPS

3. *Does the content involve a series of steps or events?*
   Yes! Examine each step or event as a potential concept and prepare a concept lesson for those steps or events which are concepts.

IDENTIFY
PARTS

4. *Does the material require identification of parts?*
   Yes! Decide if some parts should be taught as concepts and prepare a concept lesson for those which should be taught.

CHAPTER 3

STEP 2:
DEFINE THE CONCEPT

Before you can design a concept lesson, it is necessary to define the class of objects, symbols, or events that comprise the concept to be taught. The process of concept definition involves three steps: first, identify the concept name or label that will be used to identify the general class; second, identify the attributes or characteristics that are used for identification of class membership; and, third, write a concise definition for the concept.

CONCEPT NAME	*To facilitate communication, a given class of objects, events, or symbols is usually referenced by a special word or symbol.*

A concept name can take several forms. The most common form is a new word with a specialized meaning that you want the student to understand and be able to use in later work in the area.

> **Example:** simile, personification (figures of speech, from English), isolationism, imperialism (types of national policy, from social studies), finite set, disjoint set (mathematical concepts), composition, decomposition (types of chemical reactions)

Concept classes can be labeled with common words which take on a special limited meaning.

Example: half step, whole step (note intervals in music), well balanced meal (home economics)

Concept classes can be labeled with specialized symbols.

Examples: ⊥ perpendicular, // parallel (from mathematics); ⌐ resistance in Ohms (from electronics); μ 1/1,000,000 (from metric measure)

Remember: The first step in defining a concept is to identify the concept name.

ATTRIBUTES

ATTRIBUTE is a special name used to refer to the characteristics that determine whether a particular symbol or object is a member of a particular class.

A CRITICAL ATTRIBUTE is a characteristic necessary for determining class membership.

A VARIABLE ATTRIBUTE is a characteristic shared by some but not all members of the class. It is not necessary for determining class membership.

Example: Consider the concept "declarative sentence" from English composition. Some of the attributes are as follows:

(1)   a declarative sentence is one which states or asserts a fact, OR a probability, OR a possibility, OR an impossibility; *and*:

(2)   a declarative sentence is punctuated with a period (.) or an exclamation point (!) at the end; *and*:

(3)   the word order of a declarative sentence is subject → verb → complement, OR subject → verb, OR subject → verb → object, OR inverted form of one of these word orders.

A critical attribute is a necessary condition for determining class membership. If a given instance lacks a critical attribute, it cannot be a member of the class.

Example: For the concept "declarative sentence," given above, the first attribute is critical. One of these characteristics of the first attribute *must* be present, or the statement cannot be declarative.

Students may confuse variable attributes with critical attributes. It is necessary to identify the variable attributes when preparing concept lessons so that the examples can be selected to help the student clearly distinguish critical from variable attributes.

Example: In the example of a "declarative sentence" given above, the attributes listed following the first are variable attributes. An imperative sentence, for example, is punctuated with a period or exclamation point, and an exclamatory sentence is also punctuated with an exclamation point. The word orders given can also be used for imperative or interrogative sentences. All of these are potentially confusing characteristics, since a student might feel that every sentence which ends with a period or has a subject → word → complement word order is declarative.

Remember: The second step in defining a concept is to list carefully each of the critical attributes and the most common potentially confusing variable attributes.

CONCEPT DEFINITION   *A CONCEPT DEFINITION is a statement identifying each of the critical attributes and indicating how these attributes are combined.*

A CONJUNCTIVE ("AND") CONCEPT is one in which each of the critical attributes <u>must</u> *be present.*

A DISJUNCTIVE ("OR") CONCEPT is one in which any of several critical attributes can be present but all need not be present.

A RELATIONAL CONCEPT is one in which class members are defined by the temporal or spatial relationship between two or more critical attributes.

Too often definitions are incomplete. The importance of distinguishing critical from variable attributes has already been stressed. While it is essential in defining a concept to identify carefully the important critical attributes, merely listing these attributes is not sufficient. Without some indication of the relationship among these critical attributes, the definition may still be ambiguous. To be clear, you must also indicate the way these critical attributes are combined to define examples of the class.

The most common type of definition is a conjunctive or "AND" type of relationship. A conjunctive definition indicates that *all* of the critical attributes *must* be present for an instance to be of the concept class.

Examples:

Asset—a thing of value which is owned by a business.

The relationship between the two critical attributes is illustrated by the diagram at the top of the following page.

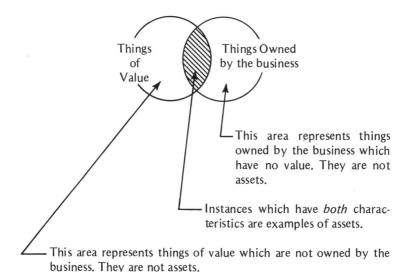

—This area represents things owned by the business which have no value. They are not assets.

—Instances which have *both* characteristics are examples of assets.

—This area represents things of value which are not owned by the business. They are not assets.

Trapezium—a plane figure with four sides, no two of which are parallel. The critical characteristics can be illustrated as follows:

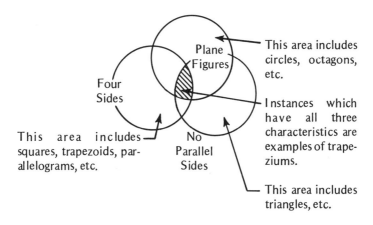

This area includes circles, octagons, etc.

Instances which have all three characteristics are examples of trapeziums.

This area includes squares, trapezoids, parallelograms, etc.

This area includes triangles, etc.

Some of the relevant nonexamples are indicated. Note that if any of the critical attributes is missing, the instance is not an example of a trapezium.

A disjunctive definition is an "OR" type of relationship. The presence of all the critical attributes is not necessary to define an example of the concept class.

Examples:

> *Declarative sentence*—a sentence which states a fact, OR a probability, OR a possibility, OR an impossibility. The characteristics can be illustrated as follows:

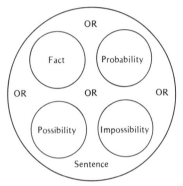

> *Strike* (in baseball)—A pitched ball at which the batter does not swing, which passes over home plate AND which is between the batter's knees and shoulders, OR any pitched ball at which the batter swings and misses. The characteristics can be illustrated as follows:

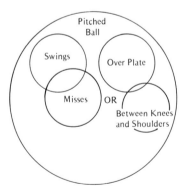

Note that this definition has both conjunctive and disjunctive characteristics. Part one requires that the pitched ball be over the plate AND that it be between the knees and shoulders. Part two requires the pitched ball to be swung at AND missed. But a strike is characterized by either part one OR part two of the definition.

A relational definition is one in which one critical attribute is the spatial or temporal relationship between two or more attributes. In other words, one attribute occurs before another, or one characteristic is positioned above, below, or within another.

Examples:

Trochaic meter (Poetry)—A line of verse or prose in which each poetic foot consists of a stressed syllable *followed* by an unstressed syllable.

In poetic meter, all meters consists of stressed and unstressed syllables. It is the pattern or temporal sequence of such stress patterns that defines the various types of meter.

Author card (Card Catalog)—The classification numbers appear in the upper left hand corner; the author's name appears first, usually offset to the left and in darker type; the title and publication information appears below the author's name.

All the filing cards, the author, subject, and title cards, have similar information. The cards can be distinguished from one another primarily by the arrangement of the information on the card.

Many definitions are compound definitions, involving several relationships among the attributes. The definition of a strike in baseball is an example of a combination conjunctive and disjunctive relationship. In stating a definition, it is often desirable to make these relationships very explicit for the student.

Remember: The third step in defining a concept is to write as concise and complete a definition of the concept as possible.

SUMMARY
STEP 2:

*DEFINE THE CONCEPT BY IDENTI-
FYING ITS NAME AND ITS ATTRI-
BUTES AND STATING A DEFINITION*

CONCEPT
NAME

1. *Identify the concept name. A concept name is a word or symbol
which is used to refer to the class as
a whole or to examples of the class.*

ATTRIBUTES

2. *List critical and variable attributes.
A critical attribute is a characteristic necessary for determining class
membership of a given instance. A
variable attribute is a characteristic
shared by some, but not all, members of the class.*

CONCEPT
DEFINITION

3. *Write a concise definition. A definition is a statement identifying each
of the critical attributes and indicating how these attributes are
combined. Definitions can specify
conjunctive, disjunctive, relational,
or combination relationships between attributes.*

CHAPTER 4

STEP 3:
COLLECT AN INSTANCE POOL

After defining the class of objects, events, or symbols to be taught, gather a large set of examples and nonexamples. The process of collecting an instance pool requires several steps. You must determine the form of representation to be used for the instances. You must collect enough instances to facilitate the development of your concept lesson.

INSTANCE

The word INSTANCE is a general term used to refer to both members and nonmembers of a concept class.

An EXAMPLE is a member of the concept under consideration.

A NONEXAMPLE is any instance which is not a member of the concept under consideration.

Example: Consider the concept adverb. The following are instances of this class of objects: (Note that sentences rather than individual words are presented because it is necessary for the student to know how the word is used in a sentence before he/she can judge whether it is an adverb.)

1.	She is *never* home.	(adverb)
2.	*Never* is a long time.	(not an adverb)
3.	The picture was painted *brightly*.	(adverb)
4.	The *bright* picture was painted.	(not an adverb)
5.	His papers are *too* messy.	(adverb)
6.	Debbie is a *sound* sleeper.	(not an adverb)

All of these words (items 1-6) are instances used in the teaching of the concept adverb. Some are members of the concept class, while others are not—but all are instances.

The word *example* used in connection with concept learning refers only to a member of the class under consideration. Be careful, however, because in everyday speech this word has many meanings. Members of a concept class are sometimes called by other names, such as: *exemplar, positive instance,* and *positive example.*

Example: In the sentences given above as instances of the concept adverb, only sentences 1, 3, and 5 are examples. The other sentences are nonexamples. All six sentences are instances.

INSTANCE
FORM

Instances can consist of the referent itself, an isomorphic representation of the referent, or a symbolic representation of the referent.

A REFERENT is the actual object, event, or symbol as it exists in the real or imaginary world.

An ISOMORPHIC REPRESENTATION is a picture, model, simulation, or other representation of the attributes of the referent in which the referent itself is not present. There is some correspon-

dence between the representation and the attributes of the referent.

A SYMBOLIC REPRESENTATION describes the referent via words or uses special symbols to stand for the referent. There may be no correspondence between the symbols and attributes of the referent.

For many concepts it is not practical or even possible to present the actual objects or events to the student. These objects or events must be represented in some way. The examples and nonexamples presented to the student to both teach and evaluate the concept are usually some representation of the actual objects or events. These forms can vary from verbal descriptions to very elaborate representations, such as full scale models or simulations.

If a given set of objects or events are usually represented in several ways, it is desirable to use all of the common types of representations in teaching the concept. If you limit the presentation and evaluation to a single type of representation, the student might acquire a misconception based on the form of representation used.

Example: Consider the concept *metaphase* as one of the five phases in the process of mitosis from biology. There are several ways to present instances that represent this process. Some of the possibilities are indicated as follows:

Slides viewed through the microscope where various types of cells are in the metaphase of mitosis (referent).

Drawings of particular organisms that are in the metaphase of mitosis (isomorphic).

Photographs taken through a microscope of actual cells in the metaphase (isomorphic).

For many concepts a wide variety of specific instances could be used to represent the concept. This is especially true of abstract concepts that represent complex ideas rather than specific sets of events or specific objects. Whenever such a concept is taught, it is necessary to specify all of the types of instances that will be used. Here, again, the wider the variety of examples used, the more adequately the student will grasp the concept and the less likely that he/she will acquire a misconception.

Example: Consider the concept "foreign policy" from social studies. This concept is a very abstract idea that can be applied to a number of different types of events or objects. It is necessary to indicate which specific types of events or objects will be included in the teaching and evaluation of this concept. Some of the types of examples and nonexamples which could be used are described as follows:

Political cartoons
Bills introduced in and/or
  passed by Congress
Speeches made by public servants
Newspaper articles
Trade agreements

For each of the above types of instances, the student would be asked to indicate whether the document or item dealt with foreign policy or with something else. A student who could correctly classify items in each of the types indicated probably has a better grasp of the concept than a student who has had experience with only one or two types.

It is important that the instance form be one that contains all of the critical attributes so that the student will be able to make an adequate classification. Sometimes instances that seem like the ideal form to use for instruction are really inadequate because they are incomplete, thus making it impossible for the student to observe the presence or absence of the critical attributes. Too often instruction uses pseudo-examples which seem to have the critical attributes but on closer examination really do not.

Example: Consider the concept *liberal* from social studies. One form of instance that might seem logical to use would be pictures of various public servants. The student would be asked to indicate whether or not the person thus identified was *liberal*. The problem with this type of example is that the student must already know a considerable amount about the person in question in order to make the judgment. None of the critical characteristics would be present in the picture. The following would be better forms for the instances to take:

> Political speeches
> Voting records accompanied by
>   abstracts of the bills involved
> Particular legislative acts

Remember: In collecting an instance pool it is necessary for you to decide the form of representation to be employed, indicate the variety of representation to be used, and eliminate any form of representation that does not adequately present each of the critical attributes to the student.

COLLECTING EXAMPLES

Having decided on the appropriate forms of representation for the examples to be collected, you should now begin to assemble your instance pool.

DIVERGENT **EXAMPLE** **RULE**	*The example pool should be as DIVERGENT as possible. Examples are DIVERGENT when their variable attributes are as different as possible.*

By *divergent* we mean that the example pool should include examples that differ from each other as much as possible while still belonging to the concept class being taught. When the variable attributes of two examples are the same or very similar, then the examples are said to be *convergent*. Examples should *not* be convergent.

1.   **Example:** Consider the concept *adverb*. Below are three examples that are *divergent*.

The plane flew *yesterday*.   (The adverb modifies the verb.)

The dinner was *not* good.   (The adverb modifies the adjective.)

She sang *very* well.   (The adverb modifies another adverb.)

In these three sentences we have illustrated three different kinds of adverbs. These examples are said to be divergent on the attribute of what kind of word is modified by the adverb.

2.   **Example:** Consider the following examples of the concept *adverb*. Are these examples divergent or convergent?

She walked *slowly* home.

Debbie slept *soundly*.

The flag waved *sadly* over the battlefield.

You should have recognized that these three adverbs are convergent. Note that all three adverbs end in -ly. An -ly ending is a variable attribute. Note that all three adverbs answer the question "how?" Note that all three adverbs follow the verb that they modify. Are the three examples, as a set, convergent or divergent with the set of examples included in the example above? Look before you read the answer!

Answer: As a set they are divergent. Note that example set 1 has no -ly endings while set 2 are all -ly ending adverbs. Note that the adverbs in set 2 all answer the question "how?" while only the third example in set 1 answer the question "how?" Note that in two of the examples in set 1 the adverb precedes the verb while all of the adverbs in set 2 follow the verb. In other words, on all of these characteristics the two sets are divergent.

3.   **Example**: Consider the concept *well defined set* from mathematics.

Definition: A set is well defined when, given a specific element, you can tell whether or not it belongs (or is contained in) the specified set.

Are the following examples of well defined sets convergent or divergent?

The first ten letters of the English alphabet.

$$\Big\{ a, b, c, d, e, f, g, h, i, j \Big\}$$

The set of letters in the word *book*.

$$\Big\{ b, o, o, k \Big\}$$

Answer: Obviously convergent. Both definitions involve letters. Students might come away thinking sets are always sets of letters.

4.   **Example**: The following are some divergent examples of the concept *well defined set.*

     The set of persons in your family
     The *Americana Encyclopedia* Set
     All male children
     All people with seven toes on one foot

All of these examples are also well defined but considerably divergent from the examples above. Note that we have introduced different kinds of objects because the type of object included in a set is a variable attribute. We have introduced an infinite set (all male children). Even though a set is infinite, it can still be well defined. We have also included an empty set (all people with seven toes . . .). Even though the set is empty we can still identify a member should we ever encounter one; hence the set is still a member of the class "well defined set." Are you beginning to get the idea of divergent examples?

5.   **Example**: Consider one more concept from science—the concept *work*.

Definition: The result achieved when a force moves an object through a distance.

Are the following examples divergent or convergent?

A boy pushing a wagon
A fork lift loading hay
A man casting a fishing line
An automatic lawn sprinkler crawling
   along its hose

Have you got it? Obviously, these examples are divergent. The variable attributes include the source of energy, the mass of the object being moved, the distance the object is moved, and the direction of the force. In the examples given we have force applied by a human moving his body in two examples while the others include water force on a gear and force supplied by a diesel engine. The objects vary from a fishing line to a bale of hay to a sprinkler. The distance and direction varies from lifting to throwing and pulling.

6.   **Example**: The following are convergent examples of the concept *work*.

A boy pulling a wagon
A horse pulling a plow
A dog pulling a sled

It is unlikely that anyone would choose such convergent examples, but these do illustrate convergence.

Remember: The example pool should be as divergent as possible.

COLLECTING NONEXAMPLES

The word nonexample used in connection with concept learning refers to any nonmember of the class under consideration. Technically, everything that is not an example is a nonexample. We must be very careful, however, because most nonexamples are not useful for concept instruction. Only nonexamples that resemble examples and hence represent a potential source of confusion for the student are useful nonexamples. Generally, when we use the word nonexample we are referring only to those instances that a student might incorrectly call an example.

The second part of Step 3 is to collect nonexamples. The following rule is a guide to assure that the nonexamples collected will assist the student to gain the desired concept when they are used in the instructional and evaluation materials which we will prepare.

MATCHED
NONEXAMPLE
RULE

For each example, collect or devise a matched nonexample. An example and nonexample are MATCHED when their variable attributes are as similar as possible.

By matched we mean that a nonexample should resemble a given example as closely as possible while still being outside of the concept class.

1. **Example**: The following adverb example and nonexample are matched.

    The book was *easily* understood.   (Example)
    It was an *easy* book to understand.   (Nonexample)

    Some of the variable attributes are the subject of the sentence, the stem word (easy), and the message of the sentence. You will note that all of these things are the same. The difference is the critical attribute, i.e., what does the word based on "easy" modify. In the first sentence easily *modifies* understood, *a verb. In the second sentence* easy *modifies* book, *a noun.*

2. **Example**: The following adverb example and nonexample are not matched.

    Slowly, she walked home.   (Example)
    The *loud* train chugged up the hill.   (Nonexample)

In this case there is little similarity between the two sentences. While a student is likely to confuse adverbs and adjectives, this particular combination differs on most of the variable attributes that are present.

3.   **Example**: Consider the concept *lever* from elementary science.

Definition: A lever is a stiff bar, not always straight, which is arranged so that it may turn about a fulcrum.

Are the following instances a matched example and nonexample?

This is a screwdriver being used to punch a hole in a can. (Nonexample)

This is a screwdriver being used to open a paint can. (Example)

Answer: Be sure you have arrived at your own answer before reading ours: This is a well matched example-nonexample pair. Note that the tool involved is the same. It is the use to which the tool is put that makes it a lever. The critical attribute is the presence or absence of a fulcrum.

4.   **Example**: Consider the concept of lever again. *Is this example-nonexample pair matched or not?*

Is this nut cracker a lever?

(Answer—Yes)

Is this ramp a lever?

(Answer—No)

Answer: Not matched.

What could you pair with a nutcracker that would provide a matched nonexample? How about the following?

Is a lever being used to crack this nut?

What are the variable characteristics used for matching?

In the following example we will attempt to illustrate both the "Divergent Example Rule" and the "Matched Nonexample Rule." The concept chosen is a more abstract concept than those used thus far and may not be as obvious. Hopefully it will help you see that the examples used are divergent from each other, while the nonexamples that are presented are matched to the examples.

Example: The concept chosen for this illustration is the concept *conservative* from a unit on political ideologies in social science.

Definition: Defenders of the king in early Britain; reluctant to change; want to preserve; those who are moderate in their thinking.

Objective: The student will be able to classify examples of political ideologies in current events items not previously used in class instruction.

Directions for the student: For each of the following quotations (#s 1 and 2), indicate whether the point of view represented is conservative or not.

#1

Alarms are being sounded about the growing interest of the government in the private lives of its citizens.
A record of every important fact about every individual in the nation, from the cradle to the grave, is gradually being built by the government.

Now there is a talk of a Federal Data Center into which all or part of this information could be fed. Here in one place could be a dossier bank on each of the nation's more than 200 million people. That bank would grow with the population and the growing volume of data on each individual.

Press a button and out could come the life story of any person, to be used for purposes of the government. Here could be tax records, records of any brushes with the law from traffic violations to indiscretions in youth or old age, school records, records of any personal transactions involving the government, and health records.

Privacy of the citizen is seen as a protection against abuse of power. And a growing number of people see proposed data banks as posing a potential threat to that privacy.

#2

No person has the right to own another person in any way, shape or form. This has been a basic doctrine of our society since it was originated. However, do we recognize the fact that a marriage contract is a form of ownership of one person over another? One day all of society will recognize this discrepancy and will do away with marriage as an out-dated carryover from the past.

True democracy depends on the absolute freedom of the individual to act as he sees fit with the consequences for his acts as the only deterrent to his behavior. Some day society will realize this idea of true democracy and on that day men will begin to be completely free!

Directions for the student: For each of the following cartoons indicate whether the point of view represented is conservative or not.

#3

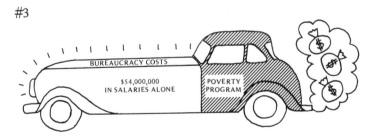

#4

Why are the examples divergent? One deals with civil rights and personal freedom while the other deals with a government program. One is a political speech or newspaper article, the other is a cartoon. The only common dimension is the critical attribute dealing with the outlook for advocating change or preserving the system.

Why are the nonexamples matched to the examples? In the first pair, both articles deal with personal freedom. Both are news articles. The difference is the point of view expressed. Perhaps they could have been matched even more closely if both had dealt with the subject of a national data bank or if both had dealt with marriage as an institution affecting freedom.

The second pair both deal with a proposed poverty program. They are both political cartoons. The critical attribute is the difference.

This concept is much less clear-cut then the others we have used for illustration. We hope that you will realize that even abstract concepts can be represented by an instance pool containing divergent examples and nonexamples.

Remember: For each example collect or devise a matched nonexample.

SOME HELPFUL HINTS

HINT   *When collecting examples and nonex-*
                              amples, use a format that is appropriate
                              for instruction or evaluation.

You can save yourself a lot of work in the long run if when you collect your instances you use the same format that will be used later when you prepare the concept lesson or a test. This means that if you need pictures, collect actual pictures, not descriptions of pictures or references to pictures. If you need newspaper articles, actually cut them out and glue them on 8½ x 11-inch sheets that will facilitate some reproduction process later.

HINT   *Get too many instances.*

You will always need extra instances. It is better to err in the direction of accumulating too many instances rather than too few. When you start to match nonexamples, you will always find that some are difficult or impossible to match. When you start to try out your instruction, you will always find that some of the instances are ambiguous or confusing to the student. When it comes to constructing a test, you will frequently wish you had enough to prepare parallel forms. In other words, get a bunch.

You are probably saying to yourself, WOW!!! Why do text books contain only one or two examples? Why don't they contain nonexamples? Why do I need instances? The answers to these questions are not easy.

For one thing, most authors are *not aware* of the principles you are learning as part of this instructional design guide. For another, texts are usually limited in size, and in order to cover a great deal of material they conserve by containing a limited number of illustrations or examples. Until very recently very few people realized the importance of nonexamples for instruction. Besides, if everyone already used these principles for instruction there would be very little necessity for you to prepare instructional materials. So gather up your big bunch of instances and whistle a little tune like "How many times (instances) have I told you."

SUMMARY STEP 3:	*COLLECT AN INSTANCE POOL OF DIVERGENT EXAMPLES EACH MATCHED TO A NONEXAMPLE*
INSTANCE FORM	*1. Decide on the form of representation to be used, indicating the variety needed and eliminating any forms which do not adequately present the critical attributes. Instances can consist of the referent itself, an isomorphic representation of the referent, or a symbolic representation of the referent.*
DIVERGENT EXAMPLE RULE	*2. The instance pool should be as divergent as possible.*
MATCHED NONEXAMPLE RULE	*3. Each example in the instance pool should be matched to a nonexample.*

CHAPTER 5

STEP 4:
ESTIMATE DIFFICULTY
FOR EACH INSTANCE

INSTANCE
DIFFICULTY

Some symbols, objects, or events in a particular concept class will be easier to classify than others. An indication of the ease with which a given instance can be classified is called INSTANCE DIFFICULTY.

In discussing the selection of items for the instance pool (Chapter 4, Step 3) we emphasized that the scope of the concept class must be represented by a full range of examples. That is, instructional examples should demonstrate a wide range of common variable attributes. In addition to obtaining a range of instances according to variable attributes, it is important to estimate the difficulty of each example. This difficulty estimate should be in reference to the students, not the teacher. Instance difficulty can be based on the ability of a sample of students to correctly identify examples from a list containing instances from several concept classes.

EMPIRICAL
ESTIMATION
OF INSTANCE
DIFFICULTY

Instance difficulty can be estimated by determining the probability of a given instance being correctly classified by a sample of students who have been given only a definition.

Selecting the concepts to be learned and the instances to illustrate the concepts has involved, so far, just the teacher. However, the teacher and student might have different interpretations of what constitutes difficulty.

Using a circle to represent a concept class, with increased distance from the circle's center indicating a higher degree of difficulty, the asterisk here represents the teacher's evaluation of one example:

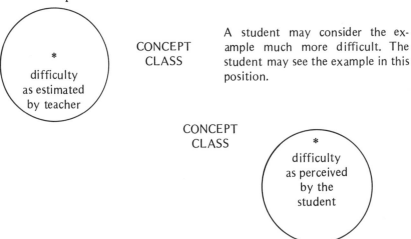

CONCEPT CLASS

A student may consider the example much more difficult. The student may see the example in this position.

CONCEPT CLASS

To be useful for instruction, instance difficulty must be estimated prior to use of the instances in the final instructional environment. An empirical rating based on the ability of a sample of students, from the target population, to correctly identify examples from a list containing both examples and nonexamples is desirable.

This empirical analysis consists of giving the students a definition of the concept and the list of (randomly sequenced) instances. Students are asked to classify each instance. The purpose of this analysis is to estimate the difficulty of the individual instances. Percentile ratings are calculated for each instance by dividing the number of correct responses by the total number of students.

The results of this instance analysis can be ordered in terms of frequency of correct responses along a continuum. Instances within the middle (30-70%) of the distribution are referred to as medium probability. Those instances correctly identified beyond the upper cut-off point (approx. 70%) are termed high probability (easily recognized), while instances below the lower cut-off point (approx. 30%) are termed low probability (difficult to recognize).

Given a concept with a fairly large number of possible instructional instances, the frequency distribution should look something like this (the actual cut-off scores can be adjusted for a given concept class):

Percent of students getting instance correct

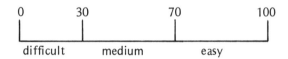

To obtain the data for the instance difficulty analysis the teacher may wish to present the instances to 30 or 40 randomly selected students. That size group should give a reasonable rating of difficulty. The sample group should be similar in intelligence and aptitude to the students who are to receive the instruction.

Perhaps the easiest way to obtain difficulty estimation is to collect the data on a given set of instances one term (or year) and then use this data for the next class. If you teach several classes in the same subject you can use one class to gather difficulty estimates for the other class. Other possibilities should occur to you.

Example: The following paragraphs illustrate the instance difficulty estimation procedure. The concept for our example is *adverb*. The procedure below describes difficulty estimation for only one concept. It is possible to use the same method when several concepts are to be learned simultaneously. In the example below we can use other forms of grammar as the nonexamples. Since we are not teaching the other forms, we use the term nonexample for instances of other grammatical forms.

The first part of the instance difficulty analysis follows what has been discussed thus far in the book. That is, determining that what is to be learned is a concept (Step 1), defining the concept verbally (Step 2; that includes identifying the critical and variable attributes), and selecting the pool of instances (Step 3).

For our illustration using the concept adverb, the definition is as follows:

> An adverb is a word that modifies a verb, an adjective, or another adverb and answers one of these questions: When? How? Where? or To what extent?

The critical attributes are: Modifies another word and function.

The variable attributes seem to be: Length of word, syntax position, frequency of usage.

Once the definition and the accompanying critical and variable attributes are specified, the instances can be selected. Recall, the purpose of clearly identifying the critical attributes is in the matching of examples with nonexamples. On the other hand, variable attributes are used in selecting divergent examples, and for making sure a range of examples is available for student learning.

In our adverb example the following instances were selected and rated by teachers as easy, medium, and difficult. Notice that the examples and nonexamples are matched, while the examples are divergent.

	Easy Examples		*Easy Nonexamples*
1.	You are *so* happy.	13.	*Sewing* makes you happy.
2.	She has been absent *lately*.	14.	She has been *late*.
3.	*Slowly*, she walked home.	15.	She is *slow*.
4.	The train chugged *loudly*.	16.	The *loud* train chugged.

Medium Examples
5. Are you *fighting* mad?
6. Clouds gathered *threateningly*.
7. It was *not* difficult to explain.

8. The *most* dangerous weapon is a gun.

Medium Nonexamples
17. Do you *fight*?
18. The *threatening* clouds gathered.
19. It is difficult to explain that *not* is a negative word.
20. *Most* guns are dangerous weapons.

Difficult Examples
9. The *small* floral print looked pretty.
10. Cats are my *No. 1* favorite pet.
11. He wants the *dark* purple bicycle.
12. The book had *three* color pictures.

Difficult Nonexamples
21. The *small* print looked pretty.
22. *One* special cat is my favorite pet.
23. He wants the *dark* trim to match.
24. The book had *three* pictures.

Instance difficulty estimation involves the collection of data from representatives of the student target population. In our empirical analysis, we presented the sentences to 110 seventh grade students after they had studied the definition. Each sentence was given a percentile score by dividing the number of correct student responses on the instance by 110. Percentages of the correct responses for the sentences listed above are as follows:

Examples   *Nonexamples*

	Examples		*Nonexamples*	
1.	68	13.	88	
2.	64	14.	89	These percentages should be
3.	84	15.	75	high (easy sentences)
4.	66	16.	60	

5.	70	17.	90	
6.	56	18.	50	These percentages should be
7.	14	19.	43	middle range (medium sentences)
8.	20	20.	5	

9.	22	21.	10	
10.	40	22.	40	These percentages should be
11.	28	23.	30	low (difficult sentences)
12.	44	24.	55	

From these results it is possible to determine the frequency distribution of both our examples and nonexamples. The frequency table can then be used to empirically place the instances into one of the three categories. There will be cases where the teacher's rating of individual instances will be different from the students'.

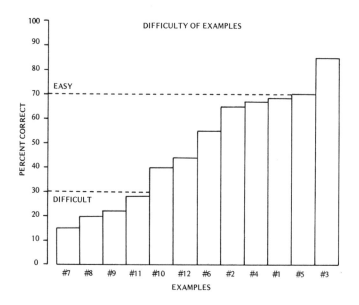

Across the bottom of the chart the sentence examples are arranged in order of difficulty and numbered as above. Using 30% and 70% as cut-off values, two examples (#3 and 5) are rated easy by the students, and four examples (#7, 8, 9, and 11) are rated difficult. There is considerable correspondence between the teacher estimates and the percentage data. Note, however, that items 7 and 8 were more difficult than the teacher thought, while items 10 and 12 were not as difficult as the teacher thought.

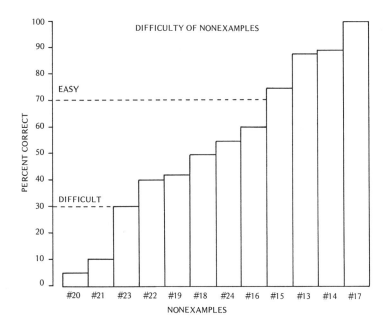

The frequency distribution for nonexamples is similar. If the discrepancy between student ratings of matched examples and nonexamples is large enough to put the example in one category and the matched nonexample in a different category, then an adjustment should be considered. Example number 7 is rated hard, its matched nonexample, number 19, is medium. In this case you may want to modify the nonexample. Overall, the correlation is good.

Rules for using difficulty ratings will be discussed in Chapter 10.

SUMMARY STEP 4:	***ESTIMATE DIFFICULTY FOR EACH INSTANCE***
INSTANCE DIFFICULTY	*1. Some symbols, objects, or events in a particular concept class will be*

easier to classify than others. An indication of the ease with which a given instance can be classified is called instance difficulty.

ESTIMATING INSTANCE DIFFICULTY

2. *Instance difficulty can be estimated by determining the probability of a given instance being correctly classified by a sample of students who have been given only a definition.*

The procedure involves a presentation of the instances with the definition to a portion of the target population. The number of correct and incorrect responses for each instance are recorded to determine what percentage of the sample identified each instance correctly. A frequency distribution of the examples demonstrates visually the range of the instances. So as not to slow down the development process, it is desirable to collect a sufficient instance pool in Step 3 to enable adjustment for differences between the teacher ratings and the student ratings.

CHAPTER 6
STEP 5:
PREPARE A DIAGNOSTIC
CLASSIFICATION TEST

CLASSIFICATION
TEST

A CLASSIFICATION TEST is an instrument which enables the instructor to make valid and reliable inferences about the student's ability to classify newly encountered instances of the concept(s).

Earlier we defined classification behavior as the ability to correctly identify the class membership of a specific symbol, object, or event. In a classroom learning situation it is appropriate to test the students to see if they can indeed perform classification behavior; that is, generalize to new examples and discriminate between instances of different concept classes. Because many concepts have an almost infinite number of instances, a classification test needs to be designed so that from a sample of instances the instructor can make inferences about each student's probable performance on newly encountered instances.

CLASSIFICATION
EVALUATION
RULE

Classification behavior is best measured by presenting students <u>newly</u> encountered examples and nonexamples of the concept class and having them identify those which are members and those which are not members.

55

Once an instance of a class has been presented to the students and identified as a member of the class, this example is no longer useful in measuring generalization. The instance is said to have been *encountered*. The second time it is presented to the students and they identify its class membership, there is no way to know whether they are generalizing or whether they are remembering the specific example. Therefore, previously unencountered or newly encountered instances are used for the testing of classification behavior. Newly encountered instances refer to instances for which class membership has not been previously identified either by or for the students.

Example (part 1): The following definitions and examples were used in instruction on two legal concepts, "hearsay" and "best evidence" rules.

Definitions:

The "best evidence" rule operates to exclude evidence or testimony relating to the contents of a written document, where:

1.   The document is itself evidence of the truth of the matter to be proved, rather than the mere recording of an assertion or statement by a person.
2.   There has been no showing as to why the original document itself is not available as evidence.

The "hearsay" rule operates to exclude testimony or evidence relating to an out-of-court statement or assertion made by a person other than the witness, where:

1.   The evidence or testimony relating to the out-of-court statement or assertion is being introduced in order to prove the truth or the statement or assertion.
2.   The truthfulness of the person in making the out-of-court statement is not certain.

On the next page are the examples for each of these coordinate concepts (see Chapter 10 for a definition of coordinate concepts). These examples were also used as part of the original instruction.

Best Evidence Rule:

Plaintiff is attempting to prove the existence of a written contract. At trial, he asks his client, whom he has called as a witness, the following:

Question: "Did you and the defendent enter into a written agreement?
Answer: "Yes."
Question: "What were the terms of the written agreement?"
Defendent's lawyer: "Objection."
Judge: "Sustained."

(Reason—the actual document would provide better evidence about the terms of the contract, and the plaintiff has not given any reason why the original document could not be provided.)

Hearsay:

Plaintiff's lawyer then tries a different approach in proving the existence of the contract by having the plaintiff relate a conversation between plaintiff and Jones, a disinterested third party, in which Jones made reference to the contract between plaintiff and defendant.

Question: "What did you and Jones discuss?"
Answer: "The stock market, and the affairs of our business."
Question: "Did you and Jones say anything about your business dealings with the defendant?"
Answer: "Yes."
Question: What did Jones say about your dealings with the defendant?"
Defendant's lawyer: "Objection."
Answer: "He congratulated me on closing the contract with the defendant."
Judge: "Sustained."

(Reason—the answer is not admissible. Jones' statement, which implied the existence of the contract and which the plaintiff is attempting to use in order to prove the existence of a contract, was made out of court.)

Because the above examples were used as part of the instruction to the student, they are "encountered" examples.

Example (part 2): In a classification test it is important to use instances which have not been used in the instruction. For our example here on legal concepts, the following is a newly encountered test item:

Identify whether the following is an example of the best evidence or hearsay rule (using the contract case from part 1):

Question: "Do you have the contract with you?"
Answer: "No, but I do have a photostatic copy of a carbon copy of the original."
Plaintiff's attorney then attempts to introduce this copy into evidence.
Defendant's laywer: "Objection."

(Answer—Best evidence rule. There has been no showing by the plaintiff of why the original can not be produced.)

Example (part 3): Too often test items simply change some of the variable attributes, allowing the students to rely on their memory of specific instances rather than on their ability to classify. The following is a previously encountered example.

Identify whatever the following is an example of the best evidence or hearsay rule (using the contract case from part 1).

A plaintiff's lawyer tries to prove the existence of a contract by having plaintiff relate a conversation between himself and Smith, a third party.

Question: "Mr. Smith and you were in discussion?"
Answer: "Yes. We were discussing some possible real estate acquisitions."
Question: "Was the contract between you and the defendant discussed?"
Answer: "Yes."
Question: "What comments did Smith make regarding the contract?"
Defendant's lawyer: "Objection."
Answer: "He thought the contract was a good deal."

(Answer—Hearsay.)

This test item is like the example used in instruction. Encoun-tered examples result in memorization not classification.

Another common inappropriate procedure used by teachers in testing concepts consists of having the students write or recognize the definition, or list the characteristics of a class. These behaviors require memorization and do not require classification behavior. Writing or recognizing a definition may be a desirable instructional outcome, but it should not be confused with understanding a concept or demonstrating classification behavior. It has been shown frequently that being able to name the characteristics of a given class does not mean that the students will be able to recognize examples of that class.

MEASUREMENT OF CLASSIFICATION BEHAVIOR   *Classification behavior can be adequately inferred only by testing students with a* range *of newly encountered instances.*

As in all test construction the validity of inference, and in this case classification behavior, requires that the students be tested with a valid *sample* of items. For classification behavior, instance validity is a function of how adequately the sample of instances represents the range of possible instances of the class. The reliability of this inference is a function of the number of instances included in the testing sample; the more instances in a test, the better the reliability. However, the *range* of instances is the most important factor in constructing a classification behavior test. Basically, a classification behavior test should be prepared with a sample of newly encountered instances that represent the range of the concept class.

Items for a classification behavior test should be selected at the same time instances for the instruction are collected. When this is done the design of the test is much easier, and there will be a ready supply of divergent and matched instances. Recall that in Chapter 4, Step 3, we said that instances should be selected in groups whereby the examples within each concept class are divergent (variable attributes that are as *different* as possible) and that the instances between classes are matched (variable attributes are as *similar* as possible). If a concept class has a wide scope of possible instances, then the test must include a larger range of instances than a test for a concept class with a smaller scope.

> **Example**: The law concepts of hearsay and best evidence rule have a range of variable attributes that can make individual instances very easy or very hard. Therefore, it is important that the instruction present sufficient instances to demonstrate the scope of each concept. It is equally important to have a range of instances on the test so that adequate inferences of student classification behavior can be made.

Some concept classes have a limited number of variable attributes or have easily recognized critical attributes. The scope of these concept classes may not include difficult examples; hence, fewer instances are necessary for the test, and fewer instances are needed in the instruction.

TYPES OF CLASSIFICATION TEST ITEMS   *Students can demonstrate classification behavior by means of a variety of question situations and test item forms, including true/false, matching, short answer, multiple choice, and short essay.*

Classification of newly encountered instances can be accomplished by using several different response forms, including true/false, matching, multiple choice, and short answer. The type of form used in the test is independent of the adequacy of the inference. Remember that there are two psychological processes involved in classification behavior: generalization and discrimination. The exam should test both of these conditions—the student's ability to *generalize* to newly encountered examples of the concept learned in instruction, and the student's ability to *discriminate* between newly encountered instances of two or more concept classes.

True/False. In many testing situations true/false items are at the memorization level of behavior. It is for this reason that true/false tests are often considered inadequate. However, when used at the classification level the true/false question can be a useful test item.

1.　**Example**: This instance is an RX_2 crystal. True or False?

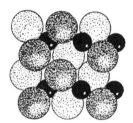

(Answer: True)

Another form of the two choice test item is the yes-no question.

2.　**Example**: Is this instance an RX_2 crystal. Yes or No?

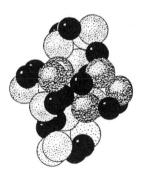

(Answer: No)

Matching. Matching questions are most appropriate when testing a number of related concepts. Given a list of instances and the names or labels of the concept classes, the students are to match the names with the newly encountered instances. This form is often used in tests of memorization, but it is very useful for testing classification.

> **Example:** The following matching test shows slides of cloud formations. The students are required to mark them A, B, C, or D from the following choices.

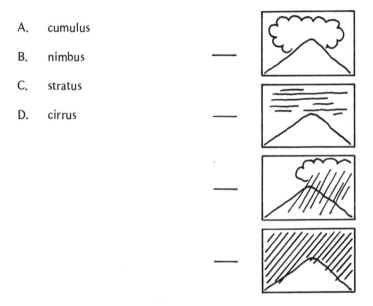

A.   cumulus

B.   nimbus   ——

C.   stratus

D.   cirrus   ——

                     ——

                     ——

Short Answer. In classifying instances it is often desirable for the student to recall the name of the concept. This type of classification behavior test question is useful if the real-world content requires recalling a name when presented a newly encountered instance. It is possible that a student could classify an instance if given the name but still not recall the name. A teacher should select short answer questions only if the student has practiced remembering the names in the instruction.

Example: When studying trees, such as in a botany class, the students must remember the concept names of the various trees, so that when presented with a newly encountered leaf they can classify the instance by giving the common name of the tree to which it belongs. Or, when seeing a new tree, the students can identify the common name, Latin name, genus, or species (or all of these concept labels) by examination of the leaves.

Multiple Choice. This type of question is an extension of the True/False question. It differs in the number of discriminations required of the students. Usually multiple choice questions require four or more choices.

Example: Which of the following sentences contains an adverb?

1. His two papers are messy.
2. She had a slow walk home.
3. She is never home.
4. Debbie is a sound sleeper.

(Answer: 3)

Short Essay. There are many concept classes that are highly influenced by interpretation. That is, individual instances can be classified in any of several ways, depending on interpretation of the attributes. In such cases the student can be asked to provide an explanation for his/her classification of the instance. Many concepts learned in secondary education and higher education, and practiced in the real world, require verbal or written interpretation of the instances. It is desirable to test such ambiguous concepts in this form. It would be inappropriate to test the students in one of the earlier mentioned forms and then to make inferences about their ability to perform interpretations.

Example: Why is this instance an example (or nonexample) of the concept of negative reinforcement?

The young boy could not attend baseball practice until he finished his homework.

(Answer: Student writes in an answer.)

Remember: In constructing a classification behavior test:

1.   *All test items should be newly encountered instances.*

2.   *Do not use definition recall or recognition as substitutes for instance classification.*

3.   *A divergent range of instances is required to insure adequate inference.*

4.   *A variety of test forms is possible.*

5.   *The test items should be sequenced randomly.*

CLASSIFICATION ERRORS

CORRECT CLASSIFICATION AND CLASSIFICATION ERRORS

CORRECT CLASSIFICATION occurs when the student correctly identifies examples as examples and nonexamples as nonexamples.

An OVERGENERALIZATION ERROR occurs when the student incorrectly identifies some of the nonexamples as examples.

*An UNDERGENERALIZATION ER-
ROR occurs when the student incorrectly identifies some of the examples as
nonexamples.*

*A MISCONCEPTION ERROR occurs
when the student incorrectly assumes
that one of the variable attributes is
critical. Consequently he/she incorrectly
identifies examples which do not have
this attribute as nonexamples and nonexamples which do have this attribute as
examples.*

In many testing situations there is only one way to assess
student responses (answers) to individual items—that is, either
right or wrong. However, in concept learning it is useful to
determine if the student is overgeneralizing (saying that nonexamples of one concept are examples of another concept),
undergeneralizing (failing to recognize an example as a member of
a particular concept class), or misconceiving (only recognizing
certain examples and nonexamples and not others as members of a
concept class). If a student has truly mastered a concept, then
he/she should be able to correctly classify almost all newly
encountered examples; but when this is not the case, it is
important to determine which type of error the student is
committing so that remedial or adaptive instruction can be given.
Therefore, for diagnostic purposes a concept test should be scored
in four different ways. Each of the scoring patterns will determine
what problems, if any, the student has. Further explanation and
examples of each of the scoring patterns follows.

    1. Correct classification. When a student really understands a
concept, he/she should be able to correctly identify all examples
as members of the class and all nonexamples as nonmembers of

the class. Correct classification is illustrated by the following figure.

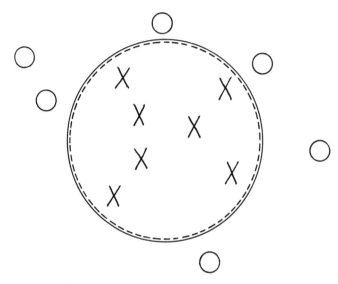

In the figure, the X's indicate examples of the concept class and the O's indicate nonexamples of the concept class. The solid circle represents the set of all class members agreed upon by the teacher or society in general. Note that, by definition, the examples (X's) must fall inside the solid circle while the nonexamples (O's) must fall outside the solid circle. The dotted circle encloses those instances that the learner indicates are members of the class. In the case of correct classification, the actual concept set (solid circle) and the set of instances said to be members by the student (dotted circle) correspond. Note that the dotted circle must be determined by inference through sampling a sufficient number of newly encountered instances (examples and nonexamples) to determine the student's response pattern.

Example: The above explanation will be easier to understand if illustrated by a specific example. Consider the following:

Concept name: Adverb

Definition: An adverb is defined as a word that modifies a verb, an adjective or another adverb and answers one of these questions: When? How? Where? or To what extent?

Test: The student is asked to indicate whether or not the italicized word in each of the following sentences is an adverb.

	Correct Answer	Difficulty
1. She has been absent *lately*.	Adverb	Easy
2. She has been *late*.	Not an adverb	Easy
3. He wants the *dark* purple bike.	Adverb	Hard
4. The *only* shirt was sold.	Not an adverb	Hard
5. The boy wants *to* go.	Not an adverb	Easy

Correct classification can be inferred if the student responds with the correct answers as indicated above. Correct classification of the concept adverb can be diagrammed as in the following figure.

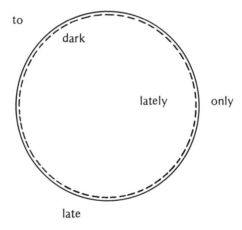

2. Overgeneralization. One category of errors is called overgeneralization. The name comes from the fact that the student fails to discriminate between classes. In a test situation the student will indicate that some of the nonexamples are in fact examples of the concept class. Overgeneralization is illustrated in the following figure.

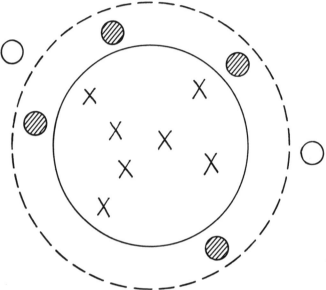

In the figure, the X's indicate examples while the O's indicate nonexamples. The solid line encloses the actual concept set. The dotted line encloses the instances that a student who overgeneralizes would include in a concept set. The shaded O's are the nonexamples that the student says are examples. Also note that when a student overgeneralizes he does not incorrectly include all nonexamples, but only those that share variable attributes with the examples.

Example: Consider the concept adverb as described above.

Overgeneralization can be inferred if the student responds with the following answers:

Italicized Word	Student's Response	Correct Response
lately	Adverb	Adverb
late	Adverb	Not an adverb
dark	Adverb	Adverb
only	Adverb	Not an adverb
to	Not an adverb	Not an adverb

Overgeneralization can be diagrammed as follows:

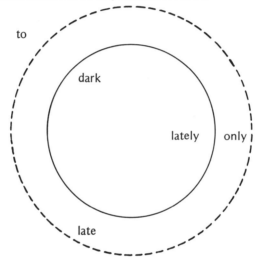

The student has failed to discriminate nonexamples from examples. He/she is indicating that any word that might possibly be
an adverb is an adverb. Since the word "to" is part of the verb it
is not likely that a student will confuse this word with an
adverb.

3. Undergeneralization. The undergeneralization error occurs
when a student fails to generalize to all of the examples that are
actually in the concept set. In a test situation a student who
undergeneralizes will indicate that some of the examples are not
members of the concept class. He/she will still indicate that all of

the nonexamples are not members of the set. Because the student is not generalizing to all members of the set, he/she is undergeneralizing. Undergeneralizing is illustrated in the following figure.

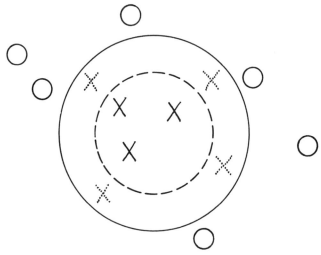

In this figure, the symbols are the same as in the previous figures. The dotted X's indicate actual examples which the student incorrectly says are nonexamples. Note that the student correctly identifies the real nonexamples as nonmembers of the class.

Example: Consider the concept adverb as described above.

Undergeneralization can be inferred if the student responds with the following answers:

Italicized Word	Student's Response	Correct Response
lately	Adverb	Adverb
late	Not an adverb	Not an adverb
dark	Not an adverb	Adverb
only	Not an adverb	Not an adverb
to	Not an adverb	Not an adverb

Undergeneralization can be diagrammed as follows:

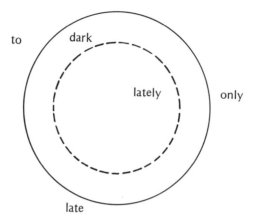

The student has failed to generalize sufficiently, and consequently has failed to label a difficult example as a member of the class. Note that he/she correctly labels the nonexamples.

4. **Misconception.** A misconception is more difficult to detect. It is called a misconception because the student thinks that a *variable* attribute is a *critical* attribute. Consequently, whenever a nonexample has this characteristic, the student thinks that it is a member of the class. Whenever an example does not have this characteristic, the student thinks that it is *not* a member of the class. In other words, the student has conceptualized incorrectly, and hence is said to have a misconception. In a test situation, two things happen. First, the student indicates that some actual examples are not members of the class. These are usually examples that do not have the characteristic the student incorrectly thinks is necessary. Second, the student indicates that some actual nonexamples are members of the class. These are usually those nonexamples that do have the characteristic that the student incorrectly thinks is necessary. Misconception is illustrated in the following figure.

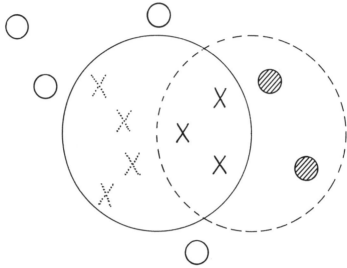

In this figure, the dotted line again encloses those instances that the student says are members of the class. The dotted X's indicate those examples that the student incorrectly says are nonexamples. The shaded O's indicate those nonexamples that the student incorrectly says are examples. He/she will correctly label the other O's and X's as nonexamples and examples.

Example: Consider the concept adverb as described above. A misconception can be inferred if the student responds with the following ansers:

Italicized Word	Student's Response	Correct Response
lately	Adverb	Adverb
late	Not an adverb	Not an adverb
dark	Not an adverb	Adverb
only	Adverb	Not an adverb
to	Not an adverb	Not an adverb

Misconception can be diagrammed as follows:

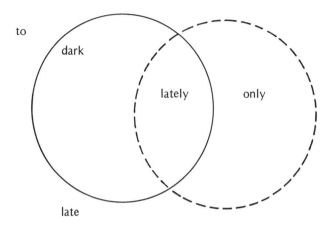

In this situation, the student has incorrectly assumed that an -ly ending is a necessary characteristic of an adverb and has, consequently, indicated that the words ending in -ly are adverbs while those which do not end in -ly are not adverbs. There are other possible misconceptions, such as word order, that might confuse the student. A different set of instances would be required to detect such errors.

SCORING THE TEST

It is possible to score a classification test four different ways. The purpose of such a scoring procedure is to assess student learning and to diagnose classification errors. Scoring the test for this diagnostic purpose can be helpful in identifying those students who require additional learning experiences for a particular concept. Recognizing the specific type of error for each student will make the additional instruction more effective and efficient.

The first step in scoring the test is to check student responses in relationship to the correct answers and the three types of classification errors.

SCORING
THE
TEST

CORRECT CLASSIFICATION—all examples and nonexamples which are correctly identified are given one point on the correct classification score.

OVERGENERALIZATION—all nonexamples which are identified as examples are given one point on the overgeneralization score.

UNDERGENERALIZATION—all examples which are identified as nonexamples are given one point on the undergeneralization score.

MISCONCEPTION—all nonexamples which share a particular variable attribute and which are identified as examples plus all examples which do not share this particular variable attribute and which are identified as nonexamples are given one point on the misconception score.

Example: The following figure illustrates the scoring procedure. In column one are the numbered instances identified as examples (eg) and nonexamples (eg). Notice that there are ten examples and ten nonexamples. We have indicated the student's answers in the next three columns. A "+" indicates that the student was correct and his score is added in the correct classification column. A "√" indicates that the student was incorrect and his error is sorted into the appropriate error column. (Misconception errors will be illustrated later.)

Test items	Correct Classification	Over Generalization	Under Generalization	Misconception
1. eg	+			
2. e̅g̅	+			
3. eg	+			
4. eg	+			
5. e̅g̅		✓		
6. e̅g̅		✓		
7. eg	+			
8. eg			✓	
9. e̅g̅		✓		
10. eg			✓	
11. e̅g̅	+			
12. e̅g̅		✓		
13. eg	+			
14. e̅g̅		✓		
15. eg	+			
16. e̅g̅		✓		
17. e̅g̅	+			
18. eg	+			
19. e̅g̅	+			
20. eg	+			
TOTAL	12	6	2	0

Responses for the three scoring schemes are totaled at the bottom of the columns. The grand total of correct classifications and overgeneralization and undergeneralization responses is equal to the total number of test questions. In our example the student had 12 correct classification answers, six overgeneralization answers, and only two undergeneralizations for a grand total of 20.

Using this scoring procedure, it is possible to diagnose the individual student's classification behavior. If the student misses one third or more of the questions, he/she has not mastered the concept; it is then desirable to determine what type of classification error has been made. If most of the incorrect responses are either overgeneralizations or undergeneralizations, it can be assumed that whichever problem has the highest score has occurred.

1. **Example**: In the previous illustration the student has an overgeneralization problem. Of the ten nonexamples the student identified six as examples. On the other hand, the student seems to be able to identify examples—missing only two of ten examples. The diagnosis is that this student has an overgeneralization error.

2. **Example**: The following illustration is for a student with an undergeneralization error. Note that five of his/her six incorrect classifications involve identifying an example as a nonexample.

Test items		Correct Classification	Over Generalization	Under Generalization	Misconception
1.	eg	+			
2.	eḡ	+			
3.	eg			✓	
4.	eg	+			
5.	eḡ		✓		
6.	eḡ	+			
7.	eg			✓	
8.	eg	+			
9.	eḡ	+			
10.	eg	+			
11.	eḡ	+			
12.	eḡ	+			
13.	eg			✓	
14.	eḡ	+			
15.	eg			✓	
16.	eḡ	+			
17.	eḡ	+			
18.	eg	+			
19.	eḡ	+			
20.	eg			✓	
TOTAL		14	1	5	0

The misconception error is more difficult to determine than over- or undergeneralization. It occurs when a student incorrectly assumes that a variable attribute(s) is critical. The most obvious variable attributes can be identified during the design of the instruction. However, this is not always possible, so it is necessary to look for possible misconceptions when diagnosing a test. When the student misses approximately equal numbers of examples and nonexamples, and these instances range in difficulty, then misconception is probably the error.

Example: In the following illustration a misconception is indicated. Note that the student has approximately equal numbers of over- and undergeneralization errors. We have consequently placed all of the errors in the misconception column and circled them.

Test items	Correct Classification	Over Generalization	Under Generalization	Misconception
1. eg	+			
2. $\overline{eg}$		✓		⊘
3. eg			✓	⊘
4. eg	+			
5. $\overline{eg}$	+			
6. $\overline{eg}$		✓		⊘
7. eg			✓	⊘
8. eg	+			
9. $\overline{eg}$	+			
10. eg	+			
11. $\overline{eg}$		✓		⊘
12. $\overline{eg}$		✓		⊘
13. eg	+			
14. $\overline{eg}$	+			
15. eg			✓	⊘
16. $\overline{eg}$	+			
17. $\overline{eg}$	+			
18. eg			✓	⊘
19. $\overline{eg}$	+			
20. eg	+			
TOTAL	12			8

If a misconception pattern occurs in the scoring profile, the nature of the misconception can sometimes be identified by a careful examination of each of the instances which were incorrectly identified by the student. Look for a particular variable attribute which is shared by all or most of the missed nonexamples. Check the missed examples to see if most or all of them are missing this variable attribute. If they are, you have identified the variable attribute which is the likely cause of the misconception.

If the above procedure does not yield a likely cause of the misconception, then it is possible that the student is merely guessing, and that his/her errors are the result of chance mistakes rather than any systematic errors. In this case additional practice with well designed instructional materials should correct the problem.

Having diagnosed the student's problem as overgeneralization, undergeneralization, or misconception, it is possible to prescribe additional instruction to help correct the problem.

CORRECTING CLASSIFICATION ERRORS

If a student makes an overgeneralization error, additional instruction should consist of matched *example-nonexample pairs with* attribute isolation *which emphasizes the absence of the critical attribute(s). If a student makes an undergeneralization error, additional instruction should consist of more* difficult *examples with attribute isolation which focuses attention on the presence of the critical attribute(s).*

If a student makes a misconception error, additional instruction should consist of matched example-nonexample

> *pairs which are <u>divergent</u> on the variable attribute causing the confusion. Attribute isolation should focus the student's attention on the noncritical nature of this variable attribute.*

Overgeneralization usually occurs because there was inadequate matching of examples to nonexamples. Where overgeneralization occurs, carefully check the matching relationships invovled. Perhaps the matching and associated attribute isolation do not adequately focus the student's attention on the difference between critical and variable attributes.

Undergeneralization usually occurs because the student did not practice with a sufficient number of difficult examples or with a wide enough range of examples. Check to be sure that the examples in the practice set include difficult instances.

A misconception usually occurs when a subset of the instances share some variable attribute(s). Check to be sure that all or most of the variable attributes have been varied in a divergent set of instances.

SUMMARY STEP 5: *PREPARE A DIAGNOSTIC CLASSIFICATION TEST*

CLASSIFICATION TEST

1. *A classification test is an instrument which enables the instructor to make valid and reliable inferences about the student's ability to classify newly encountered instances of the concept(s).*

CLASSIFICATION
EVALUATION
RULE

2.   *Classification behavior is best mea-sured by presenting students with newly encountered examples and nonexamples of the concept class and having them identify those which are members and those which are not members.*

MEASUREMENT OF
CLASSIFICATION
BEHAVIOR

3.   *Classification behavior can be ade-quately inferred only by testing students with a range of newly encountered instances.*

TYPES OF
CLASSIFICATION
TEST
ITEMS

4.   *Students can demonstrate classifica-tion behavior by means of a variety of question situations and test item forms, including true/false, match-ing, short answer, multiple choice, and short essay.*

CORRECT
CLASSIFICATION
AND
CLASSIFICATION
ERRORS

5.   *Correct classification occurs when the student correctly identifies ex-amples as examples and nonexam-ples as nonexamples. Students can also make the following classifica-tion errors:*

An overgeneralization error occurs when the student incorrectly identi-fies some of the nonexamples as examples.

An undergeneralization error occurs when the student incorrectly identi-

fies some of the examples as nonexamples.

A misconception error occurs when the student incorrectly assumes that one of the variable attributes is critical. Consequently he incorrectly identifies examples which do not have this attribute as nonexamples and nonexamples which do have this attribute as examples.

SCORING
THE
TEST

6. *Diagnostic classification tests are scored as follows:*

   a. *Correct classification—all examples and nonexamples which are correctly identified are given one point on the correct classification score.*

   b. *Overgeneralization—all nonexamples which are identified as examples are given one point on the overgeneralization score.*

   c. *Undergeneralization—all examples which are identified as nonexamples are given one point on the undergeneralization score.*

   d. *Misconception—all nonexamples which share a particular variable attribute and which are identified as examples plus all examples which do not share this particular variable attribute and which are identified as nonexamples are given one point on the misconception score.*

CORRECTING CLASSIFICATION ERRORS

7. *Additional instruction can be prescribed to overcome particular classification errors as follows:*
    a. *If a student makes an overgeneralization error, additional instruction should consist of* matched *example-nonexample pairs with attribute isolation which emphasizes the absence of the critical attribute.*
    b. *If a student makes an undergeneralization error, additional instruction should consist of more* difficult *examples with attribute isolation which focuses attention on the presence of the critical attribute.*
    c. *If a student makes a misconception error, additional instruction should consist of matched example-nonexample pairs which are* divergent *on the variable attribute causing the confusion. Attribute isolation should focus the student's attention on the non-critical nature of this variable attribute.*

CHAPTER 7
STEP 6:
PREPARE ATTRIBUTE ISOLATION

For each example and nonexample to be used in instruction, prepare an attribute isolation display.

Remember from Chapter 3, Step 2, that *attribute* is a special name used to refer to the characteristics that determine whether or not a particular symbol, object, or event is a member of a particular class. A *critical attribute* is a necessary condition for determining class membership. A *variable attribute* is a characteristic shared by some members of the class, but not necessarily by all members of the class.

ATTRIBUTE ISOLATION RULE	*Use some attention focusing device to direct the student's attention to the critical attributes present in a specific example; to potentially confusing variable attributes present in a specific example or nonexample; and to the absence of the critical attributes in a specific nonexample.*

One of the differences between an instructional environment and a natural environment is that instruction includes additional information or is structured in ways which facilitate learning. Attribute isolation is one way in which this instructional "help" is provided. As you prepare attribute isolation materials, always ask yourself the question "Does this really *help* the student to see why this particular instance is or is not a member of the concept class being taught?"

Examples: Following are several versions of the same example:

1. In the first, no attempt has been made to provide helpful attention focusing material.

    Definition: A fraction is one or more of the equal parts of a whole.

    The circle has been divided into four equal parts. Each part is a fraction of the whole circle.

    No attempt has been made to focus the student's attention on any particular attribute.

2. In this second version color (simulated here by bold type) has been added. Does it help the student to focus on critical attributes?

    Definition: A **fraction** is one or more of the equal **parts** of a whole.

    The circle has been divided into four **parts**. Each **part** is equal. Each **part** is a **fraction** of the whole circle.

    Bold type *has been used to focus the student's attention on important words. However, these words are* **not** *the critical attributes. Hence, this is* **not** *attribute isolation.*

    Be sure to identify the critical attributes and focus the student's attention on instances of the attributes.

Inappropriate attribute isolation might hinder the student. It is important to focus attention on instances of the critical attributes. Focusing attention on the concept name is usually not helpful.

Example: Shading (to simulate color) has been used in this third version also. Does it help the student see the critical attributes?

Definition: A fraction is one or more of the equal parts of a whole.

The cirlce has been divided into four parts. The (*IIIII*) parts are the same size or equal. The (∷∵∴) parts are also equal. Each (*IIIII*) part is equal to each (∴∵∴) part. Each part is a fraction of the whole circle.

The attribute being isolated is "equal parts." Shading is used to focus attention on each part and to facilitate the comparison of one part with another.

Helping students focus on potentially confusing variable attributes or to see the absence of a critical attribute is also desirable attribute isolation.

Example: Does the use of shading help the student see why this is not an example?

Definition: A fraction is one or more of the equal parts of a whole.

This circle has been divided into four parts. Is the (*IIIII*) part equal to the (∷∵∴) part? Is the (ⅢⅢⅢ) part equal to the white part? Each part is a different size. Each part is not one-quarter of the whole circle.

The attribute being isolated is "equal parts." This is a nonexample. Shading has been used to focus the student's attention on the parts and to facilitate their comparison so that he/she will realize they are not equal.

ATTENTION
FOCUSING
DEVICES

Some useful attention focusing devices include color, exploded drawings, special symbols, written or audio notes, simplified illustrations, and stop-action photography.

Often the most effective attribute isolation consists of combinations of two or more devices. Many of the examples which follow use such combinations.

Instances of a particular concept often suggest other unique ways to call attention to the critical attributes. Any procedure which catches and focuses the student's attention is acceptable. Those suggested here are only illustrative and by no means exhaust the possibilities.

COLOR

Color is one of the easiest and most effective devices used for attribute isolation. It is particularly valuable for symbol concepts but its use is by no means limited to them.

Several cautions and suggestions might help in the use of color.

(1) Don't use color or other attribute isolation techniques merely to emphasize important words. Remember the purpose of attribute isolation is to focus attention on instances of the attributes *not* on concept names or attribute names.

Example: The second version of the fraction concept, earlier in this section, illustrated the use of color (simulated by shading in this book) to emphasize important words. This is an inappropriate use of color for attribute isolation.

(2) Be sure you emphasize the critical attribute of the concept being taught. It is easy to confuse attribute concepts with related concepts. Emphasizing the wrong attribute or attributes of related concepts may hinder rather than help the student.

Example: In the following example the intended concept is iambic meter. However, the concept emphasized is metric foot. This is a prerequisite concept and as such this example is not bad; however, as shown, it does not isolate the stress pattern which characterizes an iambic foot.

Definition: An iambic metric foot is an unstressed syllable followed by a stressed syllable.

This verse has iambic metered feet.

My heart rebels **against** my gen **era** tion
That talks of free **dom and** is slave **to rich** es.
                              Santayana

Alternating bold and light type have been used to focus the student's attention on each foot. This will help the student identify the foot in a metered line, but it does not focus his/her attention on a particular stress pattern for a particular kind of foot (in this case iambic).

Be sure to identify the critical attributes and focus the student's attention on instances of these attributes.

(3) When two or more attributes are to be isolated, it is useful to use two or more colors, being careful to coordinate the color of the attribute name with the instance of the attribute as present in the instance of the concept being taught.

1. Example: In this example bold type is used to call attention to the stressed syllables.

Definition: An iambic metric foot is an unstressed syllable followed by a stressed syllable.

This case has iambic metered feet.

My **heart** re.**bels** a.**gainst** my **gen** er.a tion
That **talks** of **free** dom **and** is **slave** to **rich** es.
Santayana

Note that the author has omitted the last stressed syllable from each line.

The critical attributes are stressed syllables, unstressed syllables, and stress pattern sequence. Bold type was used to emphasize stressed syllables.

The note calls the student's attention to an exception which might confuse the student.

2.   **Example**: Color (simulated by bold type) is used in a similar way for these nonexamples of iambic meter.

Definition: An iambic metric foot is an unstressed syllable followed by a stressed syllable.

The following lines are not iambic.

Once up **on** a **mid**.night **drear**.y,
While I **pond**.ered **weak** and **wear**.y
Poe

Notice that the first syllable in each foot is stressed.

I **went** to the **gard** en of **love**
And I **saw** what I **nev** er had **seen,**
Blake

Note that the first foot is iambic but in each of the other feet two unstressed syllables precede each stressed syllable.

The critical attribute is stress pattern sequence. These verses represent nonexamples of iambic foot. Bold type is used to emphasize the stress pattern. The effective use of notes assists in focusing the student's attention on the critical attributes.

3. **Example**: In the following example, the attributes require the use of a previously learned rule (i.e., transforming the equations to slope intercept form). Attribute isolation consists of color (bold type) to call attention to the slope throughout the process of applying the rule.

Definition: Two lines are said to be parallel to one another if they have the same slope.

The equation of line 1 is:
   y - 6 = 3x

The equation of line 2 is:
   6x - 2y + 7 = 0

Remember, the **slope** intercept equation alone is:
   y = mx + b where **m = slope**

Line 1 in intercept form is:
   y = 3x + 6   **m = 3**

Line 2 in slope intercept form is:
   y = 6/2 x + 7/2
   y = 3x + 3.5   **m = 3**

Note the slopes are equal, hence the lines are parallel.

The critical attribute is slope. This slope is easily determined by reminding the student about the slope intercept form of an equation and helping him reduce the equations to this form.

Bold type is used to focus his/her attention on the part of the equations which gives the slope of the two lines.

EXPLODED DRAWINGS

In some concepts, attributes can be literally isolated by means of exploded drawings or breaking the instance apart into its attribute components. Before using this technique, be sure that an exploded drawing isolates the critical attributes. Sometimes literal isolation of the wrong components can confuse the student rather than focus his/her attention on the attributes.

Example: In the following example, the drawing has been exploded and the components rearranged. Does this help the student focus on the attribute of equal parts?

Definition: A fraction is one or more of the equal parts of a whole.

The circle has been divided into four parts.

If we cut the circle into its parts,

and compare the parts to each other,

we can see that each part is a different size. The parts are **not** equal.

Each part is **not** ¼ of the whole circle.

The attribute being isolated is "equal parts." This is a nonexample. An exploded drawing is used to isolate each part.

Usually one thinks of object concepts as candidates for exploded drawing attribute isolation. This same technique can often be used with symbol concepts.

Example: Breaking words into syllables has been combined with bold type for stressed syllables in the following example to focus the student's attention on iambic meter stress pattern.

Definition: An iambic metric foot is an unstressed syllable followed by a stressed syllable.

These words each comprise an iambic foot.

in.**vent**   re.**turn**   re.**peat**
I.**guess**   some.**times**   mean.**while**

*The critical attributes are stressed and unstressed syllables
and sequence. Bold type has been used to focus attention
on the stressed syllable. Syllables have been separated to
focus attention on sequence.*

Exploded drawings are most useful for concepts which have
attributes requiring complex visual discrimination. The components of the more complex display are much easier for the
student to identify when they are isolated from the whole.

Example: Compare the following two examples of an RX_2 crystal
structure. Chemists use drawings of spheres to illustrate structures
of various crystals. To the new student such drawings are
extremely difficult to interpret. Can you see the two-to-one
structure in the first drawing? Now look at the second drawing.
Does the attribute isolation provided help you to "understand"
the concept?

Definition: There is a type of crystal called RX_2, which has
a two-to-one ratio in its atomic structure, i.e., for a given
atom there will be two other atoms (or clusters of atoms)
attached to it in a repeating fashion.

Such structures are symbolically represented by drawings of
spheres. The color and size of such spheres represent
position and density and have nothing to do with the
structure.

In the crystal structure illustrated on the next page, there is
a repeating pattern of one small atom (R) with two larger
atoms (X_2) so it is an example. Notice that in this example
some of the outer RX_2 units are not complete. Keep in
mind that these diagrams represent only part of the total
crystal structure, and that the same patterns present in the
diagram keep repeating throughout the rest of the crystal
structure.

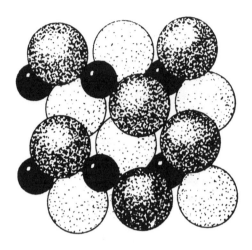

The two-to-one structure is very difficult to observe in this unprompted drawing. Many students are unable to detect it at all.

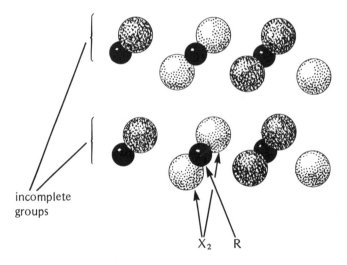

The exploded drawing plus the verbal explanation facilitates seeing the relevant characteristic in this drawing.

SPECIAL SYMBOLS

Often arrows, underlining, italics, or other symbols can be used to focus attention on the critical attributes. Some disciplines have developed special symbols which (if the student has learned them) can be used for attribute isolation.

Examples:

1. Accent marks are used in the following verse to indicate the stress pattern.

    Definition: An iambic metric foot is an unstressed syllable followed by a stressed syllable.

    This verse has iambic metered feet.

    My heart re bels a gainst my gen er a tion

    That talks of free dom and is slave to rich es.
    Santayana

    Note that the author has omitted the last stressed syllable from each line.

    The critical attribute is stress pattern sequence. The accent mark (') has been used to isolate stress pattern. Note that dividing words into syllables further assists the student to focus on stressed and unstressed syllables. The note calls attention to an exception to the rule. Often a combination of devices will provide the most adequate attribute isolation.

2. In the following sentences italics and arrows are used to call attention to critical attributes of adverbs.

    Definition: An adverb is a word that modifies a verb, an adjective, another adverb and answers one of these questions: When?, How?, Where? or To what extent?

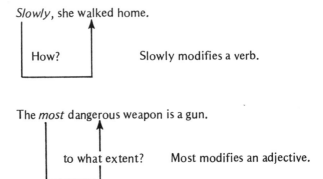

The arrow shows which word the adverb modifies. The italics focus attention on the adverb. The note identifies what kind of word is being modified.

WRITTEN OR AUDIO NOTES

One of the most used and most convenient forms of attribute isolation to use is some explanation which tells the student where to look or what to notice. Such verbal directions can be given live (in a lecture or discussion) or by means of notes (such as we've used throughout this book) or a recorded message to accompany a given display.

Example: The following illustrates appended questions which help focus the student's attention on the critical attributes of the example given. Numerous other examples of notes have been given in conjunction with other forms of attribute isolation on previous examples.

Definition: *Foreign Policy*: the actions taken by the government of one country towards another. *Domestic Policy*: the actions taken by the government of a country towards things that involve only that country.

Read the following descriptions: Which is most like foreign policy; which is most like domestic policy?

1. Mary Jo never ate potatoes because she didn't want to gain weight. She gave all of her potatoes to her sister.

   Domestic ☐
   Foreign ☐

2. Robert earned an allowance from his parents. He often spent part of his allowance on his friend David who was poor and did not have an allowance.

   Domestic ☐
   Foreign ☐

For your consideration: Did Mary Jo's actions really involve someone else? Her sister is mentioned but did her actions really involve her sister? Or was she giving the potatoes because she, Mary Jo, did not want to get fat? Her actions only really involved herself and what was best for her.

Was Roger interested in someone else? Did his actions involve someone else? His actions assisted and involved his friend.

This item is presented as a question but its purpose is to teach. It involves a type of attribute isolation which is often overlooked, that is, using a simple analogy in which the attribute is easily observed and not confounded by many variable attributes.

The questions at the end provide yet another form of attribute isolation which helps focus the student's attention on the attribute of external versus internal action.

Use of audio: Because of the print media required by this book we have printed most of the attribute isolation illustrations. Note that if this item on domestic and foreign policy was part of a workbook, the focusing questions could effectively be placed on an accompanying audio-tape. The availability of inexpensive cassette recorders makes the use of audio-tape in conjunction with a workbook an excellent delivery system which is too often overlooked. When attention-focusing directions are printed, the student must look back and forth from the directions to the display. With the directions on audio-tape, the student is able to study the display while simultaneously listening to the attribute isolation.

SIMPLIFIED ILLUSTRATIONS

Often phenomena as they appear in the real world are so complex that it is difficult to see the critical attributes which are camouflaged by an abundance of other detail. A simple line drawing which emphasizes only the critical attributes and ignores all of the extraneous detail provides valuable attention focusing help for the student.

> **Example**: The following photograph illustrates a fault. The photograph, however, is so complex that it is likely that the student will be unable to detect just where the fault lines occur. The accompanying line drawing greatly simplifies the photograph, thus enabling the student to clearly detect the fault.
>
> > *Definition*: *Fault*: a fracture along which the opposite sides have been relatively displaced. *Fault footwall*: the wall on, or boundary of, the block below an inclined fault. *Fault hanging walls*: the wall on (or boundary of) the block above an inclined fault.

This photo illustrates an inclined fault.

> This drawing shows the fault lines, the foot walls and hanging walls.

SUMMARY STEP 6:		*PREPARE ATTRIBUTE ISOLATION "HELP" FOR EACH EXAMPLE AND NONEXAMPLE.*
ATTRIBUTE ISOLATION RULE	*1.*	*Use some attention focusing device to direct the student's attention to the critical attributes present in a specific example, to potentially confusing variable attributes present in a specific example or nonexample, and to the absence of the critical attributes in a specific nonexample.*
ATTENTION FOCUSING DEVICES	*2.*	*Useful attention focusing devices include color, exploded drawings, special symbols, written or audio notes, simplified illustrations, and stop-action photography.*
CAUTIONS	*3.*	*Don't use color or other attribute isolation techniques merely to emphasize important words.*
		Be sure you emphasize critical attributes rather than variable attributes of the instance being taught.

CHAPTER 8

THE PRIMARY PRESENTATION
(RULE, EXAMPLE, PRACTICE, RECALL)

Before we can describe Step 7, the preparation of an instructional strategy, it is necessary to define the primary presentation forms from which all strategies are constructed.

Remember from Chapter 3, Step 2, that a *concept definition* identifies each of the critical attributes and how they are combined to determine class membership for a given instance. Definitions comprise the most general way to represent a concept. We often call definitions the *generality.*

Remember from Chapter 4, Step 3, that a *concept instance* is a particular object, event, or symbol which is either an *example*, i.e., member of the concept class being considered, or a *nonexample*, i.e., not a member of the class being considered.

Hence, concepts can be represented in three ways: (1) by a name or a symbol, (2) by the definition or the generality, and (3) by instances, either examples or nonexamples.

PRESENTATION FORM

Generalities (definitions and instances, examples and nonexamples) can each be presented in either expository (to tell) or inquisitory (to ask) form.

An EXPOSITORY PRESENTATION is a display which presents information but does not solicit an overt response from the student.

An INQUISITORY PRESENTATION is
a display which presents information and
solicits an overt response from the stu-
dent about this information.

When a presentation form is combined with the three ways a concept can be represented, four possible presentation forms result: Expository definition ("RULE"), Inquisitory definition ("RECALL"), Expository instance ("EXAMPLE"), and Inquisitory instance ("PRACTICE").

"RULE"—
EXPOSITORY
DEFINITION

An EXPOSITORY DEFINITION is a
display which presents the concept name
and concept definition to the student.

You are familiar with "rule" presentations. "Rule" is the form most often used in textbooks and lectures. Often the definition is not clearly isolated but must be gleaned from a paragraph or two which also states related ideas or "interesting" facts surrounding the definition. Such information may be helpful to the student if it expands or clarifies the definition.

Examples: The following examples are straightforward presentations of the definition with little or no elaboration.

1. *Definition*: Two lines are said to be parallel to one another if they have the same slope.

   Concept name is parallel lines. Critical attribute is equal slope. This is a symbol concept.

2. *Definition*: Crystals are made up of groups of identical molecules which are comprised of spheres called atoms. There is a type of crystal called RX_2,

which has a two-to-one ratio in its atomic structure, i.e., for a given atom there will be another two atoms (or clusters of atoms) attached to it in repeating fashion. The single crystals illustrated in a given diagram may not be complete in and of themselves, but remember that crystals are always symmetrical, so what you don't see may still be present.

The concept name is RX_2 crystals or RX_2 crystal structure. Critical attribute is a two-to-one ratio of atoms (with either a two cluster to one or two atoms to one being critical). The last sentence identifies a potentially confusing variable attribute so that the student will not be confused by partial sets. This is a pictorial-symbol concept where stylized drawings represent objects in the real world.

3.   *Definition*: *Fault*: A fracture in the earth's crust along which the opposite sides have been relatively displaced. *Fault Footwall*: the wall on (or boundary of) the block below inclined fault. *Fault Hanging Wall*: the wall on (or boundary of) the block above an inclined fault.

Three related concepts are being presented. Footwall and hanging wall are special names for two of the attributes of inclined faults. A single instance can illustrate all three concepts simultaneously. This is an object concept where the objects are represented by photographs.

"RECALL"— INQUISITORY DEFINITION

An INQUISITORY DEFINITION is a display which presents the concept name and asks the student to recall or recognize the definition, OR a display which presents the concept definition asks the student to recall or recognize the concept name.

In the recommended strategy to be described later, very little use is made of "Recall" presentation form. The reason is that inquisitory generalities seldom require comprehension of the concept—only memorization of the definition. There is ample evidence that remembering a definition is a poor indication of the student's ability to classify unencountered instances. Perhaps the single most prevalent instructional error is over-reliance on "recall" as an evaluation device in concept instruction. Too often it is assumed that if a student remembers or recognizes the definition, he understands the concept. This assumption is seldom justified.

The same definitions presented above in expository form are presented below in inquisitory form. Note that different types of test items have been employed. There is often a mistaken belief among instructors that a given type of test item corresponds to the degree of understanding. This is *not* the case. Almost any style of item can measure memory *or* classification. The level of behavior required depends primarily on whether the student has previously seen the definition or instance involved, not on the type of item used. All of the following "recall" displays require primarily memory level behavior; they are not good indicators of the student's understanding of the concept involved.

Example:

1. Under which of the following conditions can two lines be said to be parallel?

    a.   both lines have the same intercept
    b.   both lines have the same slope
    c.   if the lines are also congruent to each other
    d.   if the lines intersect each other at 90°.

    The student is asked to recognize the correct definition in a multiple choice format.

2. In your own words describe the atomic structure which characterizes an RX_2 crystal.

....
....
....

The student is asked to recall and restate the definition. "In your own words" encourages the use of synonyms and eliminates the need for verbatim recall. The behavior required is still memory rather than classification or comprehension. This question is short essay format.

3. Write the appropriate word in the blank space preceding the definition.

.... is the boundary of the block below an inclined fault.

.... is the boundary of the block above an inclined fault.

The student is asked to recall and state the concept names for the definitions given. This is a short answer format.

"EXAMPLE"—
EXPOSITORY
INSTANCE

An EXPOSITORY INSTANCE is a display which presents an example and/or a nonexample to the student while simultaneously identifying its concept name.

The strategy described later in this book (Chapter 9) recommends that "example presentations" be accompanied by attribute isolation. Since attribute isolation is information additional to the instance, its presence or absence constitutes a variable attribute of an expository instance presentation. The following examples represent expository instances with little or no attribute isolation.

The strategy to be described also recommends example-nonexample contrasts in expository presentation. Both single examples and contrasted examples are illustrated.

Example:

From the plot of the following equations it can be seen that they represent parallel lines.

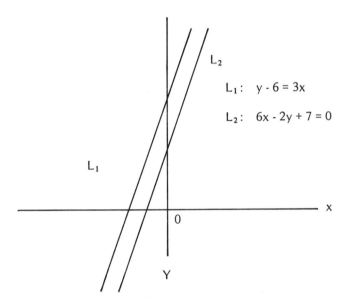

$L_1:$ $y - 6 = 3x$

$L_2:$ $6x - 2y + 7 = 0$

The instance is represented both in formula and graph form. The students are told that the lines are parallel.

When an example can take more than one form it is often desirable to present this variety to the student by displaying the same example simultaneously in different forms (as here) or by displaying subsequent examples in different forms.

This example is not contrasted with a potentially confusing nonexample.

The following expository instance consists of a contrasted example-nonexample pair of an object concept represented by stylized symbol drawings.

Example: These figures contrast a RX_2 structure with a similar structure which is not RX_2. You should be able to pick out the two-to-one arrangement in Figure 1.

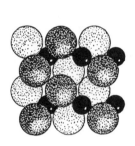 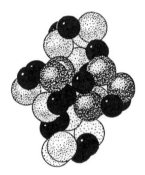

Figure 1. RX_2 crystal.

Figure 2. This crystal does not have an RX_2 structure.

Figure 1 is an example. Figure 2 is a matched nonexample. The contrast helps the student identify the critical attributes. The critical attributes are pictured in the instance. Hence, all attributes necessary for classification are present for the student to observe.

The following expository instance consists of a high fidelity representation (a photograph) of a real-world object. Both a primary concept and attribute concepts are being simultaneously illustrated.

Example: The photograph illustrates an inclined fault. The footwall block is the section to the right. The hanging wall is the section to the left. The folding of the strata and the displacement of strata layers indicate a normal fault where the hanging wall has shifted down relative to the footwall.

"PRACTICE"— INQUISITORY INSTANCE	*An INQUISITORY INSTANCE is a display which presents an example and/or nonexample and asks the student to recall or match the instance to the concept name.*

It should be obvious that inquisitory mode is similar or identical to test mode. A "practice" display is a test item. Unlike "recall" presentations, "practice" displays are the best way to assess comprehension of a given concept class, provided the instance is a previously unencountered instance.

It is sometimes useful to distinguish *practice* from *testing*. Both use inquisitory instance displays; however, practice may incorporate attribute isolation prior to responding, use matched nonexamples, and use easy → to → difficult sequences to facilitate the students' understanding. This instructional help should be systematically avoided in testing situations. (We will emphasize these points again later.)

To contrast "example" and "practice" displays, we have used the same instances in the following examples as used in the previous section. If a student had *not* already seen the expository instances, then the behavior required is classification.

Examples:

1. Following are equations for two lines. Are they parallel? Without plotting them, show why, or why not.

    $$L_1: \quad y - 6 = 3X$$

    $$L_2: \quad 6x - 2y + 7 = 0$$

    Yes   No   Why? ....

    ....

    ....

    The concept is parallel lines. Given equations (the instance form) the student is asked to point out the critical attributes or their absence as well as to answer yes or no concerning membership in the concept class. This is a modified true/false format, which is very useful for classification items.

2. For each of the following figures, indicate whether the crystal represented has an RX_2 structure or not.

    Figure 3.   yes   no   Figure 4.   yes   no

    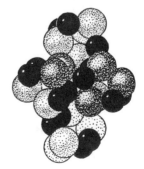

The concept is RX_2 crystals. The item format is true/false. This type of item can be extended and the guessing probability lowered by including more instances.

3. What geological formation is illustrated by the following photograph? Point out the critical characteristics and indicate how this particular formation was formed.

Formation name: ....

Characteristics: ....

....

How was it formed? ....

....

The concept is faults. The format is short essay. The student is classifying attribute concepts as well as the primary concept, fault. Unlike in the previous items this time he/she must remember (recall) the name of the concept classes involved as well as indicate class membership of the instance.

SUMMARY

THE PRIMARY PRESENTATION FORMS ARE RULE, EXAMPLE, PRACTICE, AND RECALL

PRESENTATION
FORMS

1. *Generalities (definitions) and instances (examples and nonexamples) can each be presented in either expository (to tell) or inquisitory (to ask) form. An expository presentation is a display which presents information but does not solicit an overt response from the student. An inquisitory presentation is a display which presents information and solicits an overt response from the student about this information.*

"RULE"

2. *"Rule" (expository definition) is a display which presents the concept name and definition to the student.*

"RECALL"

3. *"Recall" (inquisitory definition) is a display which presents the concept name and asks the student to recall or recognize the definition OR a display which presents the concept definition and asks the student to recall or recognize the concept name.*

"EXAMPLE"

4. *"Example" (expository instance) is a display which presents an example and/or a nonexample to the*

student while simultaneously iden-
tifying its concept name.

"PRACTICE"   5. *"Practice" (inquisitory instance) is*
a display which presents an exam-
ple and/or nonexample and asks the
student to recall or match the
instance to the concept name.

CHAPTER 9

STEP 7:
DESIGNING AN
INSTRUCTIONAL STRATEGY

DEFINITION OF
STRATEGY
PART 1

An INSTRUCTIONAL STRATEGY is a specified sequence of presentation forms.

The first step in designing an instructional strategy is to identify a sequence of presentation forms. We have defined four presentation modes: "rule" (expository definition), "example" (expository instance), "recall" (inquisitory definition), and "practice" (inquisitory instance). A single presentation of one of these four forms is an instructional display. A series of instructional displays constitutes an instructional strategy. It should be apparent that an indefinite number of strategies is possible.

In spite of the fact that a large number of strategies is possible, it has been found that some strategies are more effective than others. While it is probably unwise to try to identify "the strategy" which should always be used to teach concepts, the remainder of this chapter will describe "a strategy" which, based on instructional research, seems to be more effective than strategies which are often employed. The reader is encouraged to try a variety of strategies and to compare the strategy suggested with variations of this strategy and with other strategies he or she might observe or invent. However, based on our research and that of our colleagues the authors believe that those strategies which will prove to be most effective will resemble the one described in this chapter.

CONSERVATIVE STRATEGY: PRESENTATION FORM SEQUENCE RULE

For most students an effective strategy for teaching a correct classification of newly encountered instances consists of the following sequence: "Rule" → "example" → "practice," where "example" and "practice" are repeated (as will be illustrated later in this chapter).

This conservative strategy starts by giving the student the definition. He/she is then shown several examples, and then allowed to try to classify several more examples. This inquisitory display can be practice prior to the test or it can be used as a test or it can be both. Here we are considering it primarily as practice.

Examples: The following pages illustrate two different lessons. The first is a symbol concept, trochaic meter, from poetry. The second example is a defined concept, transfer propaganda, from social science.

These examples will be used throughout the remainder of this chapter to show the progression of completing an instructional strategy. The examples begin on the following page.

Up to this point in the text we have used smaller type and indented our examples to facilitate your study of this guide. In this chapter we are illustrating full lessons; hence our examples often require more than a single page. Consequently, while we have continued to use a smaller type, we have not indented these large examples.

This chapter requires a second format difficulty which might also confuse you. Because we are presenting full lessons, our examples contain "example" presentations within them. Our headings will appear in bold type. The examples within an example will use capital letters. Our notes about the sample lessons will appear in italics (the same style as this paragraph). Do you think you've got it? We hope so.

1. Example:

TROCHAIC METER CONCEPT LESSON

Minimal Sequence

DEFINITION:

Meter is the repeated stress pattern in a line of poetry, each repetition being called a foot. A trochaic foot consists of a stressed syllable followed by an unstressed syllable.

EXAMPLE:

> Out of childhood into manhood
> Now has grown my Hiawatha.
> (Longfellow)

PRACTICE:

If the following lines consists of trochaic metric feet check "yes." If the foot is some other stress pattern check "no."

> Now the day is over
>   Night is drawing nigh
> Shadows of the evening
>   Steal across the sky.
> (Sabine Baring-Gould)

Yes ☐   No ☐

Notes on Sample Lesson

This is a "bare bones" illustration showing the minimal number of displays necessary to exemplify the conservative strategy rule. An adequate lesson would require additional examples and nonexamples as will be illustrated later in this chapter. To avoid confusion, we have also eliminated almost all elaboration. In a real-world lesson you might add additional explanation to the definition, or you might include additional explanation to accompany the examples. In chapter 10, we have provided a lesson with this additional elaboration.

2. Example:

TRANSFER PROPAGANDA CONCEPT LESSON

Minimal Sequence

DEFINITION:

Audio: One of the types of propaganda frequently used is *transfer propaganda*. Note that there are three primary characteristics: (1) an emotion producing idea or symbol, (2) an associated idea or product, and (3) a lack of natural relationship between the two. Study the definition. (Pause).

EXAMPLE:

Audio: This advertisement is a good example of transfer propaganda.

(Example 2 continued on next page)

PRACTICE:

Audio: On your answer sheet circle A or B for the ad you think uses transfer propaganda. Write why in the space provided.

ANSWERS

1. A B Why? ....
....
....

Notes on Sample Lesson

In an attempt to illustrate various media as well as strategy, the displays for this lesson are photographs reproduced from slides. The text is the transcript of the audio track for this tape/slide presentation. Like the previous example, this is the minimum number of displays required to implement the strategy.

The practice item does not use attribute isolation but is a deviation from the recommended strategy in that the matched example/nonexample pair does provide instructional help. Early practice in matching assists the student. Matched pairs should not be used throughout practice since the student will come to rely on the contrast and be less able to classify a non-contrasted example or nonexample.

DEFINITION OF STRATEGY PART 2

***Strategy is a specified sequence of presentation forms* INCLUDING THE USE OF ATTRIBUTE ISOLATION.**

Remember, in Chapter 7, Step 6, attribute isolation was defined as attention-getting devices used to focus the students' attention on the critical attributes in a specific example, on potentially confusing variable attributes in a specific example or nonexample, and on the absence of the critical attributes in a specific nonexample. An effective instructional presentation involves the use of attribute isolation. While it is possible to have a strategy without any attribute isolation as in the previous examples, a more effective strategy utilizes this instructional help.

Sequence affects the function of attribute isolation. Thus instructional help can be presented simultaneously with an "example" or "practice" presentation or following such presentations.

PROMPTING	*PROMPTING is attribute isolation presented simultaneously with an instance in either expository or inquisitory form.*

The word *prompting* is often used to refer to devices which hint at or help the student make a correct response. This is more appropriately called *response prompting*. Simultaneous presentation of attribute isolation, however, focuses a student's attention on the critical attributes of the instance and helps him or her discriminate examples from nonexamples. Attribute isolation also helps him or her identify potentially confusing variable attributes. This attention focusing type of prompting is called *stimulus prompting*.

FEEDBACK	*FEEDBACK is attribute isolation presented following a student response (either right or wrong) on a "practice" display.*

The word *feedback* is sometimes synonymous with right-wrong information (*knowledge of results*). Our use of the term *feedback* refers to attribute isolation rather than to knowledge of results. Often on "practice" displays it is better to isolate the attributes and have the student try to respond again rather than telling him whether he was right or wrong. In this guide we will consider knowledge of results (K of R) as separate from feedback. Either or both may be used for a particular feedback display.

As with presentation form sequence, there are innumerable ways to incorporate attribute isolation into a given strategy. Again there is probably no one strategy that is universally effective. The following paragraphs describe, and the examples illustrate, a strategy for use of instructional help that has proved to be effective in many situations. The reader is again encouraged to experiment, but is advised to use the recommended strategy as a baseline for comparison.

CONSERVATIVE STRATEGY: ATTRIBUTE ISOLATION RULE	*Most students will learn to classify newly encountered instances of a concept with fewer errors and in less time if a conservative sequence incorporates attribute prompting on "example" displays and attribute feedback following "practice" displays.*

It is not always obvious to a student why a given example belongs to a particular class. If, however, the critical attributes are clearly indicated, the student is more likely to see why the example is an example. In practice, attribute isolation feedback helps the student see why his or her classification was correct or incorrect.

Examples: On the following pages the trochaic meter concept lesson and the transfer propaganda lesson are expanded to include attribute isolation. These are still minimal lessons with single instances.

1. Example:

TROCHAIC METER CONCEPT LESSON

Minimal Sequence with Attribute Isolation

DEFINITION:

Meter is the repeated stress pattern in a line of poetry, each repetition being called a foot. A trochaic foot consists of a stressed syllable followed by an unstressed syllable.

A stressed syllable is the one that is accented when spoken. In most situations, secondary accents are also considered as stressed syllables when determining poetic meter.

EXAMPLE:

Out of   **child**.hood   **in**.to   **man**.hood

Now has   **grown** my   **Hi**.a   **wath**.a.
                    (Longfellow)

PRACTICE:

If the following lines consist of trochaic metric feet check "yes." If the foot is some other stress pattern check "no."

> Now the day is over
>   Night is drawing nigh,
> Shadows of the evening
>   Steal across the sky.
>   (Sabine Baring-Gould)

Yes ☐   No ☐

(Example 1 continued on next page)

FEEDBACK:

Bold type and vertical lines are used to illustrate the stress pattern in this verse. Did you recognize the feet and identify the correct pattern?

Now.the | **day**.is | **ov**.er

Night.is | **draw**.ing | **nigh,**

Shad.ows | **of**.the | **eve**.ning

Steal a | **cross**.the | **sky**.

Each line has 3 trochaic feet except that lines 2 and 4 stop on the stressed syllable (only half of the foot is used). This stop on the stress is called a masculine ending. Did this confuse you?

Notes on Sample Lesson

An expanded definition has been included in this version of the sample lesson. This is a form of instructional help which helps the student to recall attribute definitions or points out potentially confusing variable attributes (see Chapter 3, Step 2).

Attribute isolation is accomplished by using dots to divide single words within a foot into syllables, using bold type for stressed syllables, and putting a vertical line between each foot.

The "practice" display is not prompted, but is followed by feedback in which dots separate syllables, bold type indicates stress, and vertical lines separate poetic feet. The student is not told whether he or she is right or wrong.

It is necessary for the student to study the feedback to find an indication of the correct answer. Merely saying "right" or "wrong" enables the student to skip the feedback thus failing to benefit from the information.

To find meter a student must first find the individual syllables, then must determine which are stressed, then must decide which two or three syllables constitute a foot, and finally must observe the stress pattern within a foot. The attribute isolation provided does the first three of these steps for the student by separating the syllables of a word within a foot with dots, indicating the stress by bold face, and dividing the feet by vertical lines. The student has only to observe the pattern of stress in a helped example.

2. Example:

TRANSFER PROPAGANDA CONCEPT LESSON

Minimal Sequence with Attribute Isolation

DEFINITION:

Audio: One of the frequently used types of propaganda is *transfer propaganda*. Note the three primary characteristics: (1) an emotion producing symbol or idea, (2) an associated idea or product, and (3) lack of a natural relationship between the two. Study the definition. (Pause)

EXAMPLE:

Audio: This advertisement is a good example of transfer propaganda. An emotion producing symbol, the girl in the bikini swim suit, is paried with a product, *Yankee Heritage* after-shave lotion. Since the girl is not the user of the products, there is not a natural relationship between the girl and the products. Obviously the inference (or transfer) is that the use of the products attracts beautiful girls.

(Example 2 continued on next page)

PRACTICE:

Audio: On your answer sheet circle A or B for the ad you think used transfer propaganda. Write in the space provided.

ANSWERS

1. A   B   Why? ....
....
....

FEEDBACK:

Audio: You should have noticed that the girl in the *Gold Tan* ad is illustrating the results of using the product, *Gold Tan Suntan Lotion*. This constitutes a natural relationship. While some transfer is obviously involved, the propaganda technique used here is not primarily transfer.

The *Star Pen* ad, on the other hand, pairs a beautiful girl in a swim suit with a pen. Even the caption suggests lack of any connection. The intent is for the positive emotional response produced by the "beauty" to somehow transfer to your feelings for *Star* pens.

Attribute isolation is provided by means of the audio track which identifies examples of the attributes and explains the relationship involved. The feedback is provided by providing audio after the student has responded to the practice display.

DEFINITION OF STRATEGY PART 3

Strategy is a specified sequence of presentation forms including the use of attribute isolation and ATTRIBUTE MATCHING.

Remember, in Chapter 4, Step 3, it was suggested that the examples collected as part of the example pool should be as divergent as possible. Examples are divergent when their variable attributes are as different as possible. It was also suggested in Chapter 4, Step 3, that for each example one should try to find a matched nonexample. An example and nonexample are matched if their variable attributes are as similar as possible while differing only in the presence of critical attributes.

In the strategies described and illustrated thus far, only a single display has been used in expository and inquisitory mode. If a student is to adequately acquire correct classification behavior, several instances should be presented in each mode. As with previous strategy parameters, there is an indefinite number of possible relationships between series of examples. The relationship described has been found to be effective with most students. The reader is again encouraged to experiment and compare alternatives with the relationships described.

CONSERVATIVE STRATEGY: ATTRIBUTE MATCHING RULE

Most students will make fewer errors in classifying newly encountered instances of a concept if in "example" presentations (1) each example is matched to a nonexample and (2) each example-nonexample pair is divergent from previous and subsequent pairs, and if in "practice" presentations (3) each display consists of an example or nonexample which is unmatched and divergent from previous and subsequent instances.

Why does attribute matching facilitate performance? Often it is not the definition you remember but rather an example. Thus it is easy to remember a noticeable attribute even if it happens to be irrelevant to the classification. When a nonexample is matched to the example it enables the student to compare and to observe that this noticeable attribute is common to both the example and the nonexample. Later, when trying to classify new examples, both the example and the nonexample will be rememberd. Consequently, the attribute will also be remembered as irrelevant, thus avoiding a classification error.

In practice, however, the continued use of matching provides a hint to the student. He/she is not forced to remember what was critical and what was not. Therefore, it is desirable to discontinue the use of attribute matching in the practice presentation.

Why does divergence facilitate performance? Divergence enables a student to compare an example with a different example and to see that the same critical attributes can be embedded in a wide range of variable attributes. Later when he or she sees a newly encountered example, which has still different variables attributes, the student is more likely to consider the possibility that it might be an example, even though it appears different from the examples previously seen. Thus, the probability of a correct classification is increased.

In practice it is desirable for the student to experience a wide variety of examples, hence divergence should also characterize practice even though matching should be discontinued.

> **Examples**: The trochaic meter lesson is again repeated, but additional instances, both examples and nonexamples, have been added to provide attribute matching. The attribute isolation is continued as prescribed for the new instances. This lesson is an extended sequence. It is probably more effective than the minimal sequence, but its effectiveness could be increased by further considerations, to be presented later in this chapter.
>
> The transfer propaganda concept lesson is also repeated here, with additional instances to provide for attribute matching.

1. Example:

TROCHAIC METER CONCEPT LESSON

Extended Sequence with
Attribute Isolation and Attribute Matching

DEFINITION:

Meter is the repeated stress pattern in a line of poetry, each repetition being called a foot. A trochaic metric foot consists of a stressed syllable followed by an unstressed syllable.

A stressed syllable is the one that is accented when spoken. Dictionaries mark preferred accents by this symbol (´); secondary accents (″) are also considered as stressed syllables in most situations.

EXAMPLES:

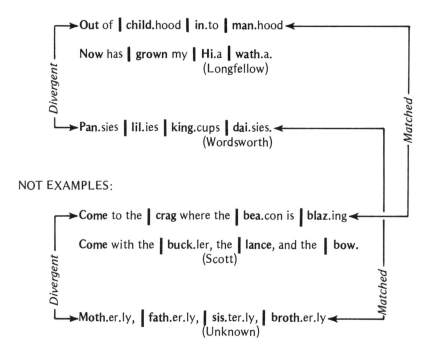

NOT EXAMPLES:

(Example 1 continued on next page)

PRACTICE:

If the following lines consist of trochaic metric feet check "yes."

If the foot is some other stress pattern check "no."

> 1. Now the day is over
>   Night is drawing nigh,
>   Shadows of the evening
>   Steal across the sky.
>   (Sabine Baring-Gould)

   Yes ☐   No ☐

FEEDBACK:

Bold type and slash marks are used to illustrate the stress pattern in this verse. Did you recognize the feet and identify the correct pattern?

> 1. **Now** the | **day** is | **ov**.er
>
>   **Night** is | **draw**.ing | **nigh**,
>
>   **Shad**.ows | **of** the | **eve**.ning
>
>   **Steal** a | **cross** the | **sky**.
>   (Sabine Baring-Gould)

The second and fourth lines end in the middle of a foot on the stressed syllable. This is a masculine ending. Did this confuse you?

PRACTICE:

> 2. Through the noises of the night
>   She floated down to Camelot.
>   (Tennyson)

   Yes ☐   No ☐

(Example 1 continued on next page)

FEEDBACK:

2. **Through the | nois.es | of the | night**

    She | float.ed | down to | Cam.e | lot.
    (Tennyson)

The fourth foot (night She) extends across the end of the first line to the beginning of the next. This verse also ends on a stressed syllable. Did these unusual patterns confuse you?

PRACTICE:

3. The sun that brief December day
    Rose cheerless over hills of gray.
    (Whittier)

    Yes ☐   No ☐

FEEDBACK:

3. **The sun | that brief | De.cem | ber day**

    Rose cheer | less ov | er hills | of gray.
    (Whittier)

This is opposite of trochaic meter. The verse starts with an unstressed syllable.

PRACTICE:

4. If the heart of man is depressed with cares
    The mist is dispelled when a woman appears.
    (Gay)

    Yes ☐   No ☐

(Example 1 continued on next page)

FEEDBACK:

4.   If the **heart** | of **man** | is de.**pressed** | with **cares,**

      The **mist** | is dis.**pell'd** | when a **wo** | man ap.**pears.**
                     (Gay)

Did this verse confuse you? It uses a mixed meter. Feet numbers 2 (of man), 4 (with cares), and 5 (the mist) all have two syllables, the rest have three. None, however, are trochaic feet.

Notes on Sample Lesson

The definition is an expanded definition. It is often helpful to define some of the critical attributes for the student. For some students this elaboration may still be insufficient. They may require a separate concept lesson on syllables. Our evaluation (see Chapters 11 and 12) will help us determine if we need an additional lesson.

In the first pair, both instances have the same topic, both express a thought, both use two lines of verse for a single sentence. In the second example/nonexample pair each consists of four words, neither expresses a thought, both are one line. While each example/nonexample pair is matched the two pairs are quite different from each other.

Attribute isolation has been provided by use of bold type, vertical lines, and dots as in previous examples.

In the "practice" presentation instances are presented one by one. No prompting is provided prior to the response. In an actual presentation, practice and feedback would appear on separate pages. We have included both on a single page here to save space and reduce costs.

In practice, feedback should follow each response. In a test you should hold feedback until the student has responded to the whole set.

The second practice item differs in several ways from the first. Potentially confusing to the student is the continuation of meter from line one to line two. Like item 1 it also involves a masculine ending. The third practice item is a nonexample. Most students find iambic (the pattern of this verse) extremely confusing with trochaic since both involve a two syllable foot. The fourth practice item is also a nonexample. This gives the student a chance to discriminate on alternating meter from a regular trochaic.

2. Example:

TRANSFER PROPAGANDA CONCEPT LESSON

Extended Sequence with
Attribute Isolation and Attribute Matching

DEFINITION:

Audio: One of the frequently used types of propaganda is transfer propaganda. Note the three primary characteristics: (1) an emotion producing symbol or idea (2) an associated idea or product (3) and lack of a natural relationship between the two. Study the definition. (Pause)

EXAMPLE:

Audio: (show left slide) This advertisement is a good example of transfer propaganda.

Audio: (show right slide—leave left up) This advertisement is not primarily an example of transfer propaganda.

(Example 2 continued on next page)

Audio: The *Yankee Heritage* ad uses an emotion producing symbol, the bikini-clad girl, paired with a product, shave lotion. Since the girl is not the user of the product, there is not a natural relationship between the girl and the products. Obviously, the inference (or transfer) is that use of the product attracts pretty girls.

Audio: The *Freedom Light* ad also uses a pretty girl to advertise a product. In this ad, however, the girl is the user. Hence, there is a natural relationship, making this a questionable example of transfer propaganda.

EXAMPLE:

Audio: (show left slide) This political cartoon is a good example of transfer propaganda.

Audio: (show right slide—leave left up) This political cartoon is not an example of transfer propaganda.

Audio: In the cartoon on the left Uncle Sam frowning and the broken piggy bank are emotion producing symbols. They are paired with an idea, Johnson's State of the Union message. Depending on your politics you might debate about the natural relationship, however, the symbols are used primarily for effect, making this a good example of transfer propaganda.

Audio: In the right cartoon there are no emotion producing symbols. The cartoon is really only an illustration of the clever caption; this cartoon does not utilize transfer propaganda.

(Example 2 continued on next page)

PRACTICE:

Audio: On your answer sheet circle A or B for the ad you think uses transfer propaganda. Write why in the space provided.

ANSWER

1.   A   B   Why? ....
....
....

FEEDBACK:

Audio: You should have noticed that the girl is illustrating the results of using the product—*Gold Tan Lotion*. This constitutes a natural relationship. While some transfer is obviously involved, the propaganda technique used here is not primarily taught.

Audio: The *Star Pen* ad, on the other hand, pairs a beautiful girl in a swimsuit with a pen. Even the caption suggests lack of any connection. The intent is for the positive emotional response created by the "beauty" to somehow transfer to your feelings for *Star* pens.

(Example 2 continued on next page)

PRACTICE:

Audio: On your answer sheet indicate whether this ad represents transfer propaganda by circling yes or no and writing why.

ANSWER

2.   Yes   No   Why? ....
....
....

FEEDBACK:

Audio: The emotion producing idea present in this advertisement is women's rights. It is paired with a product, New Day cigarettes. There's little direct relationship, but the company hopes the "right to smoke" will become part of the equality idea.

(Example 2 continued on next page)

PRACTICE:

Audio: On your answer sheet indicate whether this ad represents transfer propaganda by circling yes or no and writing why.

ANSWER

3.   Yes   No   Why? ....
....
....

FEEDBACK:

Audio: An emotion producing symbol, a girl in a bathing suit, is paired with a company, The Paper Corp. If you thought paper bathing suits are a principal product and the girl is demonstrating the bathing suit, then you might say this is a natural relationship and hence not transfer propaganda. On the other hand, if you know that The Paper Corp. is much better known for household paper products such as paper towels, toilet paper, etc., then you can see that this ad is a case of transfer propaganda, since it is these other paper products that the company is trying to sell, not the paper bathing suits.

(Example 2 continued on next page)

Notes on Sample Lesson

For the "example" presentation, both slides are presented simultaneously on two screens. (This could be sequential but visual comparison in this case is very helpful to the student.) Simultaneous presentation is used to contrast an example and a matched nonexample. The audio is used to provide attribute isolation.

The Johnson cartoon example/nonexample pair is divergent from the previous pair in many ways. Yankee Heritage and Freedom Light were both advertisements; the Johnson examples are political cartoons. This eliminates "being an advertisement" as a critical attribute. The example in the first pair associates an emotion producing object with a product; in the cartoons the symbols are associated with an idea or set of ideas. In the first pair both the example and the nonexample used sex appeal. In the second pair no sex appeal was involved.

The first instances in practice are a matched example and nonexample. The contrasted pair, as explained earlier, provides instructional help to the student.

The feedback audio is presented after the student responds. In practice this feedback should follow each response. In a test situation the student should respond to a series of items prior to getting feedback for each item.

For purposes of presentation we have placed the practice and feedback item on a single page. In the actual presentation of this concept the feedback audio would not be provided until after the student had given his/her response. If feedback is presented simultaneously with the practice, we have an "example" display rather than a "practice" display.

The second "practice" item is not matched to a nonexample, this is a divergent item because a product is paired with an emotion producing idea (woman's rights) rather than a symbol.

The third "practice" example is a much more difficult item. In previous items "why" allowed the student to indicate critical attributes thus providing a check on his choice, limiting the possibility of chance responding. Here, however, the item can be either yes or no depending on his why. The feedback for the third practice item indicates that either choice is correct depending on the reason for making the choice.

DEFINITION OF STRATEGY PART 4

Strategy is a specified sequence of presentation forms including the use attribute isolation, attribute matching, and a **RANGE OF DIFFICULTY.**

Remember in Chapter 5, Step 4, it was suggested that instance difficulty should be estimated by an empirical procedure where instances are presented to a sample of students who are asked to classify them given only the definition. Not only does the relationship of examples to other examples and nonexamples in a given concept lesson affect ability to classify, but the relationship of examples to a given population of students (i.e., instance difficulty) also affects learning. As with other rules prescribed in this chapter, the following recommendation has been based on research data; however, it should be considered as *a* suggested procedure, not *the* procedure. The reader is encouraged to manipulate instance difficulty in his/her own concept lessons and to observe the outcomes. This procedure will provide a possible starting place.

CONSERVATIVE STRATEGY: INSTANCE DIFFICULTY RULE

Most students will learn to classify newly encountered instances of a concept with less difficulty if a conservative strategy incorporates an easy to hard difficulty sequence on "example" presentations and a random sequence on "practice" presentations.

If all easy instances are used, students will be unable to classify more difficult examples when they are encountered on tests or in the real world. Usually a student who has been trained on easy instances thinks that more difficult instances are nonexamples. Hence, he/she makes the error of *undergeneralization*.

If all hard instances are used, the task is made difficult for the student and he/she becomes discouraged. If hard items aren't carefully matched to nonexamples and if only hard items are included, the student will make the error of *overgeneralization*. The combination of matched example/nonexample pairs and presentation of easy to hard instances helps overcome overgeneralization errors.

Since an easy to hard progression in practice provides a form of instructional help not likely to be found in the "real world" it is advisable to not deliberately sequence difficulty in practice.

> **Example**: The trochaic meter concept lesson is repeated here. Additional example/nonexample sets have been added to the example presentations and to the practice presentations to increase the range of difficulty available.

TROCHAIC METER CONCEPT LESSON

**Extended Sequence with Attribute Isolation,
Attribute Matching, and Adjusted Difficulty**

DEFINITION:

Meter is the repeated stress pattern in a line of poetry, each repetition being called a foot. A trochaic metric foot consists of a stressed syllable followed by an unstressed syllable.

EXAMPLES: NOT EXAMPLES:

    no.where   in.**vent**

    Fri.day   ab.**surd**

    tree.house   I.**guess**

    res.o | lu.tion   af.**fil** | i.ate

    un.der | **cur.**rent   un.der.pro | **duc.**tion

(Example lesson continued on next page)

EXAMPLE:

1.   **Out** of **| child**.hood **| in**.to **| man**.hood

   Now has **| grown** my **| Hi**.a **| wath**.a
        (Longfellow)

NOT AN EXAMPLE:

2.   **Come** to the **| crag** where the **| bea**.con is **| blaz**.ing

   Come with the **| buck**.ler, the **| lance** and the **| bow.**
        (Scott)

EXAMPLE:

3.   **Pan**.sies, **| lil**.ies, **| king**.cups, **| dai**.sies.
        (Wordsworth)

NOT AN EXAMPLE:

4.   **Moth**.er.ly, **| fath**.er.ly, **| sis**.ter.ly, **| broth**.er.ly.
        (Unknown)

EXAMPLE:

5.   **There** they **| are** my **| fif**.ty **| men** and **| wo**.men,

   Nam.ing **| me** the **| fif**.ty **| poems** un **| fin**.ished!

NOT AN EXAMPLE:

6.   'Tis **hard | to say | if great | er want | of skill**

   Ap.pear **| in writ | ing or | in judg**.ing **| ill.**

        Words such as *'tis, to, if, -er,* and *of* are not stressed
        because they do not carry the message as do stressed
        syllables.

(Example lesson continued on next page)

EXAMPLE:

7. **Tasks in | hours** of **| in**.sight **| willed**

   Can **| be through | hours** of **| gloom** ful **| filled.**
   (Arnold)

> The fourth foot (willed Can) is continued across the end of the first line to the beginning of the second. This is an unusual pattern and can be confusing.

NOT AN EXAMPLE:

8. My **mind |** to **me |** a **king |** dom **is.**

   Such **pre |** sent **joys |** there.**in |** I **find.**
   (Dyer)

> This is the opposite of trochaic. The first syllable is unstressed and the second is stressed.

PRACTICE:

For each of the following words or phrases check "yes" if the meter is trochaic and "no" if it is not.

	YES	NO	
1.	☐	☐	return
2.	☐	☐	whatsoever
3.	☐	☐	sometimes
4.	☐	☐	resurrection
5.	☐	☐	yesterday
6.	☐	☐	habituate
7.	☐	☐	summer

(Example lesson continued on next page)

FEEDBACK:

	YES	NO	
1.	☐	☑	re.**turn**
2.	☑	☐	**what**.so | ev.er
3.	☐	☑	some.**times**
4.	☑	☐	res.ur | **rec**.tion
5.	☐	☑	yes.ter.day
6.	☐	☑	ha.**bit** | u.**ate**
7.	☑	☐	**sum**.mer

PRACTICE:

	YES	NO
8.	☐	☐

           Now the day is over
                Night is drawing nigh
          Shadows of the evening
              Steal across the sky.
                  (Sabine Baring-Gould)

FEEDBACK:

	YES	NO
8.	☐	☐

    Now the \| **day** is \| ov.er
      Night is \| **draw**.ing \| **nigh**
  Shad.ows \| of the \| **eve**.ning
      Steal a \| **cross** the \| **sky**.

PRACTICE:

	YES	NO
9.	☐	☐

    If the heart of man is depressed with cares,
    The mist is dispelled when a woman appears.
             (Gay)

(Example lesson continued on next page)

FEEDBACK:

> YES   NO

9. □   □   If the **heart** | of **man** | is de.**pressed** | with **cares,**

     The **mist** | is dis.**pelled** | when a **wo** | man ap.**pears.**

Did this verse confuse you? It uses a mixed meter. The second (of man), fourth (with cares), and fifth (the mist) feet all have two syllables, the rest have three. None, however, are trochaic feet.

PRACTICE:

> YES   NO

10. □   □   I want to know
     what is really
     going on.
                (Resendez)

FEEDBACK:

> YES   NO

10. ☑   ☑   I **want** | **to** know   or   **I want** | **to** know

     What is | **real.**ly

     Go. ing | **on.**

The ordinary prose sound of this verse make the recognition of the meter very difficult. The first line is probably not trochaic. Two possible stress patterns are given. The last two lines are probably trochaic.

Notes on Sample Lesson

Previous sample lesson instance were lines of verse. It is easier to detect meter in a single word. Therefore, single word instances are included to provide easier instances for the student.

(Example lesson continued on next page)

Bold type, vertical lines, and dots were again used for attribute isolation.

The second set of single word instances is more difficult in that multiple syllable words are involved. This also makes it divergent from the first set. Divergence is often linked with difficulty, the addition of variable attributes often makes a divergent instance more difficult.

The measured difficulty (% of the student sample who misclassified instances given only the definition) for a group of college sophomores on the first four verses (unprompted) are as follows: Longfellow-25%, Scott-38%, Wordsworth-26%, and Unknown-36%.

As you can see, the examples are divergent but of approximately the same difficulty level.

The second set of verses are more difficult. Their measured difficulty was as follows: Browning-53%, Pope-43%, Arnold-41%, and Dyer-60%.

The nonexample of iambic (unstressed-stressed) meter might seem easy; however, very similar attributes are easily confused, thus making these verses more difficult.

Single word instances are provided as part of practice. As a group they are somewhat easier than verses, hence we have an easy to difficult sequence in practice rather than a completely random sequence. Grouping the single word instances and verses together seemed more logical, hence we deviated from the rule slightly.

Empirical difficulty of the first practice verses for a sample of college sophomores was as follows: Sabine Baring-Gould-17%, Tennyson-47%, Whittier-58%, Gay-37%, and Resendez-75%.

For your convenience the correct responses are indicated in feedback. In an actual situation it may be desirable not to indicate correct answers, thus encouraging the student to read all of the feedback.

For purposes of presentation, we have placed some of the practice and feedback items on the same page. In the actual presentation, the feedback should not be presented until after the student has responded to the practice item. If feedback is presented simultaneously with practice, the display is really an "example" display rather than "practice."

The last practice example is a very difficult item because the reader can put different stress on the first line depending on his interpretation of the verse.

SUMMARY STEP 7:	*DESIGN AN INSTRUCTIONAL STRATEGY*
STRATEGY DEFINITION	*1. An instructional strategy is a specified sequence of presentation forms including the use of attribute isolation, attribute matching, and a range of difficulty.*
PRESENTATION FORM SEQUENCE RULE	*2. Conservative strategy: presentation form sequence rule. For most students an effective strategy for teaching correct classification of newly encountered instances consists of the following sequence: "Rule → example → practice" where "example" and "practice" are repeated as required by other strategy rules.*
ATTRIBUTE ISOLATION RULE	*3. Conservative strategy: attribute isolation rule. Most students will learn to classify newly encountered instances of a concept with fewer errors and in less time if a conservative sequence incorporates attribute prompting in "example" displays and attribute feedback following "practice" displays.*
ATTRIBUTE MATCHING RULE	*4. Conservative strategy: attribute matching rule. Most students will make fewer errors in classifying newly encountered instances of a concept if in "example" presenta-*

tions (1) each example is matched to a nonexample and (2) each example-nonexample pair is divergent from previous and subsequent pairs, and if in practice presentations (3) each display consists of an example or nonexample which is unmatched and divergent from previous and subsequent instances.

DIFFICULTY RULE

5. *Conservative strategy: instance difficulty rule. Most students will learn to classify newly encountered instances of a concept with less difficulty if a conservative strategy incorporates an easy to hard difficulty sequence on "example" presentations and a random sequence on "practice" presentations.*

CHAPTER 10

TEACHING COORDINATE CONCEPTS

Thus far in this book we have treated concepts as isolated entities. Most concepts, however, do not exist in isolation but rather as part of a set of related concepts. Concepts can have subordinate, superordinate, and coordinate relationships with one another. Concept instruction will be more effective if these relationships are carefully considered while designing concept lessons. In this chapter we will define the rules which we have presented for teaching a single concept to more adequately reflect the relationships among concepts.

CONCEPT TAXONOMY	*A concept taxonomy is a diagram which is constructed to indicate the subordinate, superordinate, and coordinate relationships among a set of related concepts.*

Example: The following is a partial taxonomy for concepts related to poetic feet.

---

*In 1975, at the University of Minnesota, an informal conference was held with Herbert J. Klausmeier, Susan M. Markle, Philip W. Tiemann, and the authors. The materials in this chapter reflect some of the ideas discussed at this conference. The authors gratefully acknowledge the contribution of their colleagues, while accepting responsibility for this interpretation.

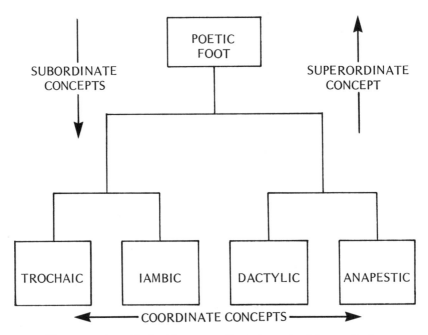

The concept poetic foot is superordinate to each of the particular kinds of feet. The concept iambic is subordinate to the concept poetic foot. The concepts iambic, trochaic, dactylic, and anapestic are coordinate.

A concept taxonomy should not be confused with an objectives hierarchy. An objectives hierarchy indicates what a student needs to be able to do as a step before he/she will be able to perform a subsequent step. There is no implication of prerequisite relationships of this type in a concept taxonomy. It is often possible to teach a coordinate set of concepts from the middle of a concept taxonomy without teaching the subordinate concepts or more than the immediate superordinate concept.

COORDINATE CONCEPTS   *When a superordinate concept is divided into subordinate concepts, the subordinate concepts for a single superordinate concept are called coordinate concepts.*

Previously we defined critical attributes as necessary conditions for determining class membership and a variable attribute as a characteristic shared by some, but not all, members of the class. Given a concept taxonomy it is possible to be somewhat more precise in our definition of concept attributes.

CONCEPT ATTRIBUTES	*CRITICAL ATTRIBUTES are those characteristics which are used to discriminate instances of coordinate concepts from one another.*
	NECESSARY ATTRIBUTES are those characteristics that characterize members of the superordinate concept and are hence necessary for identification but which do not discriminate instances of coordinate concepts from one another.
	DEFINING ATTRIBUTES are both the critical and the necessary attributes.
	VARIABLE ATTRIBUTES are the critical attributes of a set of coordinate concepts which are subordinate to the concept being taught by a given lesson.

Previously we defined variable attributes in terms of what they were not. It is less confusing to define them in terms of subordinate concepts. The definition of necessary attributes will also facilitate our definition of a definition in the next section.

Example: The following is a partial taxonomy for concepts related to poetic feet. If the purpose of the lesson is to teach the concepts trochaic and iambic then the critical, necessary, and variable attributes are as follows:

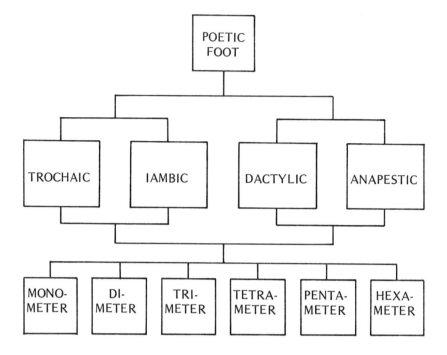

Definition: Trochaic meter is a poetic foot (necessary attribute) consisting of two syllables, the first syllable being stressed (critical attributes).

Definition: Iambic meter is a poetic foot (necessary attribute) consisting of two syllables, the second syllable being stressed (critical attributes).

A given verse may have one (monometer), two (dimeter), etc., feet. This is a variable attribute. As far as determining what type of meter is involved, this is an irrelevant characteristic. Knowing the subordinate variable attributes, however, is very helpful when selecting instances.

In Chapter 3, Step 2, we indicated that a concept definition was a statement identifying each of the critical attributes and indicating how these attributes are combined. The following is a refinement of that definition.

**CONCEPT
DEFINITION**

A concept definition identifies the superordinate concept (hence identifying the necessary attributes) and states the critical attributes and how these attributes are combined in order to define the coordinate concept classes.

Example: The components of the following definitions have been indicated.

Definition: *Dactylic meter* (concept name) is a poetic foot (superordinate concept) consisting of three syllables in which the first syllable is stressed (critical attributes).

Definition: *Trapezium* (concept name) is a four-sided figure (superordinate concept) in which no two sides are parallel (critical attribute).

In Chapter 4, Step 3, we indicated that instances selected for the instance pool should be as divergent as possible. Divergent means that the variable attributes are as different as possible. For teaching coordinate concepts this instance selection rule can also be refined.

**INSTANCE
SELECTION
RULE**

Instances should be selected so that the variable attribute possibilities are adequately represented. Nonexamples should be selected from among the examples of coordinate concept classes (close-in nonexamples). Some nonexamples should be selected from the examples of coordinate concepts once removed (far-out nonexamples).

In selecting a divergent set of instances, be sure to select instances from each of the subordinate concept classes so that the values assumed by the variable attributes are different. If there is a large number of different subordinate concepts and hence a wide number of different variable attribute values, then some representative sample is sufficient.

In dealing with coordinate concepts, the examples of one coordinate class are nonexamples for each of the other coordinate concepts. Hence the selection of an instance pool does not really consist of gathering examples and nonexamples but rather in gathering examples of each of the coordinate classes. These examples should be matched on the variable attributes shared by the various coordinates.

It is often desirable to provide practice in discriminating far-out nonexamples. A far-out nonexample is an example of a coordinate concept once removed. A coordinate concept once removed is illustrated by the following taxonomy.

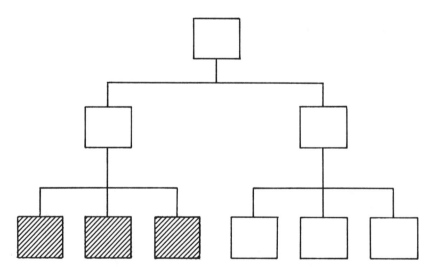

If the shaded coordinate concepts represent the classes being taught, then an example from one of these classes is a coordinate concept once-removed.

Example: Consider again the poetic meter taxonomy.

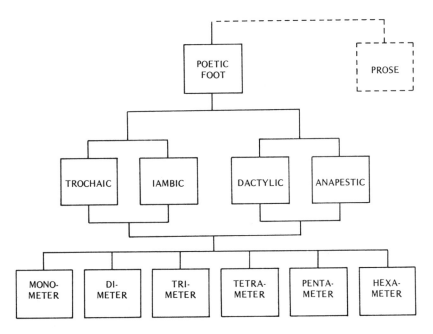

Examples should be selected for each type of meter. These examples should consist of verses (a verse is a single line of poetry or metered prose) which vary in the number of feet in the line. Examples are hence divergent on the variable attribute of number of feet. Other subordinate concepts (not shown) include tone and subject matter. Examples should also be divergent on these variable attributes. If the instances to be used are stanzas rather than verses, then rhyme scheme also becomes a variable attribute which should be systematically sampled.

A far-out nonexample would be a nonmetered line of prose in which there is no systematic meter.

In Chapter 6, Step 5, we indicated how to construct a diagnostic test to measure correct classification and the classification errors of undergeneralization, overgeneralization, and misconception for a single concept. The following procedure indicates how to construct a diagnostic test for three coordinate concepts.

The extension of this procedure to any set of two or more coordinate concepts should be easy to determine from the procedure and example given.

DIAGNOSTIC TEST FOR COORDINATE CONCEPTS

Select approximately equal numbers of easy and hard examples from each of the coordinate concept classes.

Select several far-out nonexamples from coordinate concepts once removed.

The instances should be arranged in random order using either a short answer or matching format.

Since the examples of one coordinate concept are nonexamples for each of the other coordinate concepts, it is unnecessary to select nonexamples except for a few far-out nonexamples from coordinate concepts once removed. Arranging the instances in random order serves to eliminate any deliberate matching and to minimize the inclusion of undesirable prompts to the student. If the test is merely to measure correct classification, then the proportion of examples from each coordinate concept need not be equal. However, in order to construct and score a diagnostic test, it is necessary to have approximately equal numbers of easy and hard examples from each coordinate concept.

Example: The following is a partial test for the four types of poetic meter. This example is designed to illustrate the format for a coordinate concept test but does not have a complete set of instances as prescribed above.

Test on Poetic Meter

For each of the following stanzas indicate the predominate form of meter by writing the name in the blank to the left.

....   The sun that brief December day
                      Rose cheerless over hills of gray.
                                        (Whittier)

....   I went to the garden of love
                      And I saw what I never had seen
                      A chapel was built in the midst,
                      Where I used to play on the green.
                                        (Blake)

The following is an alternate format using multiple choice instead of short answer.

Test on Poetic Meter

For each of the following verses indicate the predominate form of meter by checking the appropriate column on the left.

IAMBIC	TROCHAIC	DACTYLIC	ANAPESTIC	OTHER	
□	□	□	□	□	There are many who say that a dog has his day. (Thomas)
□	□	□	□	□	The land was ours before we were the land's. (Frost)
□	□	□	□	□	I saw the sky descending black and white. (Wilber)
□	□	□	□	□	Come to the crag where the beacon is blazing. (Scott)

In Chapter 6, Step 5, we indicated how to arrange and score instances on a test for a single concept so that you could detect specific types of classification errors—overgeneralization, undergeneralization, and misconception. A similar procedure is used to score a diagnostic test for coordinate concepts. For coordinate concepts, however, the over- and undergeneralization errors can be more adequately specified.

SCORING A DIAGNOSTIC TEST FOR COORDINATE CONCEPTS

A correct classification score for each coordinate concept is the number of examples of that concept correctly classified. The total correct classification score is the sum of the correct classification scores for each coordinate concept plus the number of far-out nonexamples correctly classified.

Errors can be sorted into N(N-1) specific classification errors (where N = the number of coordinate concept classes). If A, B, and C represent coordinate concepts, then the following classification errors are possible:

(1) Undergeneralization A, overgeneralization B

(2) Undergeneralization A, overgeneralization C

(3) Undergeneralization B, overgeneralization A

(4) Undergeneralization B, overgeneralization C

(5) Undergeneralization C, overgeneralization A

(6) Undergeneralization C, overgeneralization B

> *Undergeneralization on concept A occurs when examples are classified as examples of concept B or C, etc.*
>
> *Overgeneralization on concept A occurs when examples of concept B or C are classified as examples of concept A, etc.*
>
> *Misconception occurs whenever a student makes both under- and overgeneralization errors as a result of considering one or more variable attributes critical.*

The overgeneralization-undergeneralization relationships identified above are perhaps more easily visualized via the following diagrams.

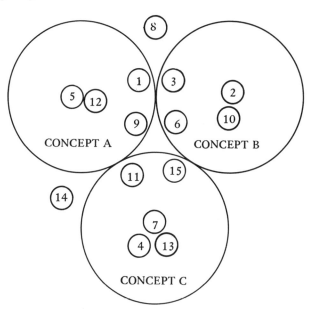

The numbers indicate test items and correspond to the numbers of the test items in the following example. Items 8 and 14 represent far-out nonexamples which are not included in the coordinate concepts A, B, or C. If a student classifies item 9 as an example of concept B, he has simultaneously undergeneralized on concept A and overgeneralized on concept B. If a student classifies item 15 as an example of concept B, he has simultaneously undergeneralized on concept C and overgeneralized on concept B; and so forth for other simultaneous under- and overgeneralization errors.

Misconception errors are more difficult to detect. Suppose that a student makes the following errors: item 8 is classified as concept B; items 9 and 15 as B; item 3 as A. These errors may represent a specific misconception if items 8, 9, and 15 share a variable attribute which is not shared by item 3. If such an attribute cannot be identified, the error pattern may be the result of guessing rather than a specified misconception.

Determining classification errors may seem unnecessary. However, this diagnosis enables the instruction to be revised in ways that are specifically designed to eliminate the errors. Even though the design procedures described in this guide are carefully followed, it is still possible to build systematic errors into the instruction. Unless a diagnostic test is constructed and administered, it is often impossible to identify the source of the trouble. A carefully constructed diagnostic test, on the other hand, not only pinpoints the difficulty but also provides a prescription to remedy the problem.

Example: The following table represents a test for three coordinate concepts labeled A, B, and C. The first column shows the item numbers (they correspond to the diagrams above). The second column shows the correct response for each item. The third column shows a sample student's responses. The remaining columns indicate the scoring procedure for this student. A "+" indicates that the student was correct and his score is added in the column shown. A "√" indicates that the student was incorrect and his/her answer is marked according to the approrpiate error.

Item number	Correct response	Student response	Correct classification A	Correct classification B	Correct classification C	Correct classification Far-out nonexamples	Under A over B	Under A over C	Under B over A	Under B over C	Under C over A	Under C over B	Misconception
1	A	A	+										
2	B	B		+									
3	B	C								✓			
4	C	C			+								
5	A	A	+										
6	B	C								✓			
7	C	C			+								
8	X	X				+							
9	A	A	+										
10	B	B		+									
11	C	C			+								
12	A	A	+										
13	C	C			+								
14	X	X				+							
15	C	C			+								
			4	2	5	2				2			

Total Correct
=13

Total Errors
=2

Note: X = far-out nonexample. The student represented in the preceding table did fairly well except that he or she confused examples of concept B with examples of concept C. The best way to remediate this condition is to provide practice using carefully matched instances from concepts B and C.

Scores from a second student are illustrated by the following table.

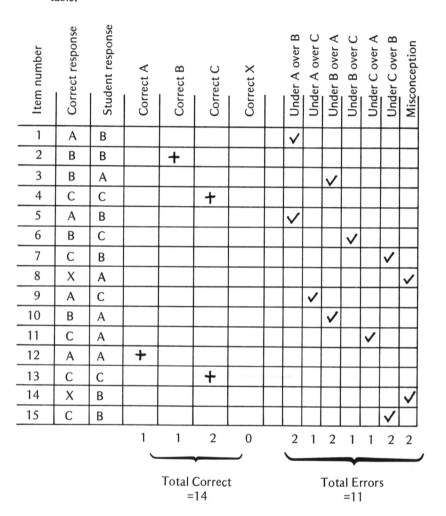

Item number	Correct response	Student response	Correct A	Correct B	Correct C	Correct X	Under A over B	Under A over C	Under B over A	Under B over C	Under C over A	Under C over B	Misconception
1	A	B					✓						
2	B	B		+									
3	B	A							✓				
4	C	C			+								
5	A	B					✓						
6	B	C								✓			
7	C	B										✓	
8	X	A											✓
9	A	C						✓					
10	B	A							✓				
11	C	A									✓		
12	A	A	+										
13	C	C			+								
14	X	B											✓
15	C	B										✓	
			1	1	2	0	2	1	2	1	1	2	2

Total Correct
=14

Total Errors
=11

Note: X = far-out examples. This student did rather poorly. From an examination of his/her error patterns there does not seem to be a consistent type of error. He/she may have some misconception but in all likelihood the errors represent random guessing. The best way to remediate this condition is to provide additional examples and practice as specified in this guide.

In Chapter 9, Step 7, it was suggested that a conservative presentation form sequence rule was "rule → example → practice." When one is teaching coordinate concepts this presentation form sequence rule can also be redefined.

PRESENTATION FORM SEQUENCE RULE FOR COORDINATE CONCEPTS	*When a set of coordinate concepts is being taught, an effective strategy for most students consists of the following sequence: $rule_1$ → $rule_2$ → $rule_3$ → $example_1$ → $example_2$ → $example_3$ → $practice_1$ → $practice_2$ → $practice_3$, where the example and practice presentations are repeated as necessary to provide attribute matching and divergence.*

This rule suggests that when teaching coordinate concepts one should first present each of the definitions. The example presentation should consist of examples of each of the coordinate concepts carefully matched and divergent on variable attributes. The practice presentation should provide an opportunity for the student to discriminate a divergent set of examples of each of the coordinate concepts from each other.

In Chapter 9, Step 7, it was also suggested that a conservative attribute matching rule was as follows: in example presentations each example should be matched to a nonexample and each example-nonexample pair should be divergent from previous and subsequent pairs. It was also suggested that on practice presentations each display should consist of an example or nonexample which is unmatched and divergent from previous and subsequent instances. As with the presentation form sequence rule, this rule can also be refined for the teaching of coordinate concepts.

ATTRIBUTE
MATCHING
RULE FOR
COORDINATE
CONCEPTS

Most students will make fewer errors in classifying newly encountered instances of coordinate concepts if in "example" presentations a series of divergent matched-example sets is presented to the student. A matched-example set is one example from each of the coordinate concepts which have been matched on the most important variable attributes. Where possible each matched example set should be presented simultaneously to facilitate comparison by the student. On practice presentations a divergent set of examples from the various coordinate concepts should be randomly sequenced to avoid undesirable prompts.

This rule is very similar to the attribute matching rule discussed in Chapter 9, Step 7, except that instead of an example/nonexample pair we now have a set of N examples (where N is the number of coordinate concepts which have all been matched with each other).

The attribute isolation rule for coordinate concepts is very similar to the attribute isolation rule stated in Chapter 9, Step 7.

ATTRIBUTE
ISOLATION
RULE FOR
COORDINATE
CONCEPTS

Most students will make fewer errors in classifying newly encountered instances of coordinate concepts if in "example" presentations attention focusing devices are used to direct the student's attention to the critical attributes for each example and if these devices direct the student's attention to how the values of the critical attribute change from one coordinate concept to the other.

This is essentially the same as the attribute isolation rule in Chapter 9, Step 7, except that when one is teaching coordinate concepts the attribute isolation should direct attention to the change in the critical attribute from one example to the next.

The difficulty rule for teaching coordinate concepts is the same as the difficulty rule for teaching a single concept.

INSTANCE DIFFICULTY RULE FOR COORDINATE CONCEPTS	*Most students will learn to classify newly encountered instances of coordinate concepts with less difficulty if a conservative strategy incorporates an easy-to-hard difficulty sequence in "example" presentations and a random sequence in "practice" presentations.*

In the case of coordinate concepts each succeeding matched-example set should be more difficult in the same way that each example-nonexample pair is more difficult when one is teaching a single concept.

Example*: The remainder of this chapter is a sample lesson designed to teach a student to identify the meter involved in a stanza or verse of a poem. The coordinate concepts are iambic, trochaic, dactylic, and anapestic.

---

*The authors adapted some of their examples from Clement Wood, *Poet's Handbook*, Garden City Publishing, Garden City, New York, 1942. Also used was Robert Frederick Brewer, *The Art of Versification and the Technicalities of Poetry*, John Grant, Edinburgh, 1918.

SAMPLE LESSON

Types of Poetic Meter

PURPOSE:

The purpose of this lesson is to teach you how to determine the different types of rhythmic patterns that distinguish poetry from ordinary prose. You will learn to recognize and name four different rhythmic patterns.

BACKGROUND:

A major feature of poetry that distinguishes it from more ordinary prose is the arrangement of words so that the stressed syllables tend to occur at regular intervals. This regular arrangement of stress produces a rhythmic pattern. It is this rhythmic pattern that is one major factor distinguishing poetry from prose.

A *stressed syllable* is louder and/or higher in pitch than an unstressed syllable. *Rhythm* in poetry results from a recurring pattern of stressed and unstressed syllables. (*The attributes of stressed and unstressed syllables are* **necessary** *attributes for types of meter.*)

Because rhythmic patterns recur, it is possible to break a poem down into rhythmic sections called "**feet.**" Each poetic **foot** (as considered in this lesson) consists of one stressed syllable plus one or two unstressed syllables. Other types of rhythmic feet are also found in verse. For this lesson, however, we will limit our consideration to feet as defined. (*The attributes of poetic feet are* **necessary** *attributes for types of meter.*)

In Chapter 9 we placed notes on sample lessons at the end of the lesson. Because of the length of this sample lesson we have inserted notes to you throughout the lesson. These notes will appear in italics of the same style as this note. Sometimes (as on this page) short notes will be placed in parentheses immediately following the part of the lesson which is being commented upon.

Previous sample lessons have been "bare bones" lessons in order to clearly illustrate the rules we were presenting. So that you won't get the idea that lessons should be so lean, we have presented a more complex lesson as a sample of an effective strategy for teaching coordinate concepts. In this lesson we have provided elaboration for the definitions which further defines the concept attributes and suggests a procedure for using the definitions to classify examples.

DEFINITIONS:

In this lesson we will be concerned with four different kinds of poetic feet: iambic, trochaic, anapestic, and dactylic.

The four kinds of stress patterns to be taught can be represented by the following table:

	STRESSED SYLLABLE FIRST	STRESSED SYLLABLE LAST
TWO SYLLABLES	**dai**.ly TROCHAIC	her **glance** IAMBIC
THREE SYLLABLES	**Praise** to the DACTYLIC	in.ter.**vene** ANAPESTIC

Notes on Sample Lesson

The table is used to help the student see the relationships between the critical attributes. Bold type is used as attribute isolation in the **imbedded** *examples.*

A *TROCHAIC FOOT* consists of a stressed syllable followed by an unstressed syllable. A single foot is called a TROCHEE.

An *IAMBIC FOOT* consists of an unstressed syllable followed by a stressed syllable. A single foot is called an IAMB.

A *DACTYLIC FOOT* consists of a stressed syllable followed by two unstressed syllables. A single foot is called a DACTYL.

An *ANAPESTIC FOOT* consists of two unstressed syllables followed by a stressed syllable. A single foot is called an ANAPEST.

The definitions have been presented twice on this page, once in table form and once as verbal statements. It is often desirable to use alternative forms for presenting the definition. One student might understand one form while another might find the other form easier to grasp.

HINT:

To help you remember which is which, remember that the words "trochaic" and "dactylic" both have a consonant as the first letter and both have the stressed syllable first. On the other hand, the words "iambic" and "anapestic" start with vowels and they have the stressed syllable last.

This hint is a mnemonic aid to help the student keep the names straight.

HELP:

The following procedure will help you detect the stress pattern in poetic verse.

First. Read the poem. Emphasize the stressed syllables. It is often helpful to mark those that are stressed.

Second. Divide each line into feet. This can be done by drawing a line between each foot. If the first syllable is stressed, draw a line before each stressed syllable. If the second or third syllable is stressed, draw a line after each stressed syllable. To produce a regular pattern it is sometimes necessary to group the natural stresses in a forced way.

Each line starts with a foot. Sometimes a partial foot with only one syllable will occur, particularly at the end of a line.

    Go and | catch a | fall.ing | star

    The fall | ing flow | er

Third. Decide which pattern is used for each foot.

Sometimes a verse or stanza will use mixed meter. For this lesson, if most of the feet are of one type classify the verse or stanza as that type of meter.

Notes on Sample Lesson

Even though they know the definition it is not always obvious to the student how to use the definition to classify instances. This page provides a guide to the student to help him/her apply the definition. Several common exceptions are also identified for the student.

The previous three pages constitute the "rule" presentations of this lesson. Note however that some examples have been imbedded in the "rule" presentation to clarify the definitions or exceptions to the definitions.

EXAMPLES:

The following words illustrate each of the four types of meter. The bold type is used to help you see which syllable is stressed. Syllables of single words within a foot are separated by dots. Feet are separated by vertical lines.

TROCHAIC: stressed-unstressed.

> A majority of the two-syllabled words in English are trochees. Some examples are:

A.dam	**das**.tard	**jaunt**.y
ar.rant	**doub**.le	**ken**.nel
a.vid	**fat**.al	**long**.er
bel.ly	**gar**.ish	**mat**.ed

IAMBIC: unstressed-stressed.

> There are not as many words in English that constitute iambs. Some examples are:

a.**bove**	de.**cree**	ma.**roon**
ac.**quaint**	en.**gage**	o.**pague**
be.**hind**	fa.**tigue**	re.**new**
be.**tray**	im.**pale**	sa.**lute**

DACTYLIC: stressed-unstressed-unstressed.

> There are many dactylic words in English. Some examples are:

bat.tle.ment	**ed**.i.ble
glut.ton.y	**car**.ni.val
fas.cin.ate	**laz**.i.ly

ANAPESTIC: unstressed-unstressed-stressed.

> English words which may be used as anapests are not as frequent. Some examples are:

ap.per.**tain**	in.ter.**fere**
dis.af.**firm**	su.per.**cede**

Trochaic and iambic examples are matched in that both include two feet. Dactylic and anapestic are matched in that both are single words, one foot. One-word instances are easiest to classify.

EXAMPLES:

Not only are single words used to produce a particular rhythmic pattern but often two or more words are combined to produce a particular type of metric foot. The following examples illustrate each of the four patterns produced from such combinations of words.

TROCHAIC: stressed-unstressed.

    Some combinations include:

boy and	**went** to
men as	**wild** as
with the	**in** the

IAMBIC: unstressed-stressed.

    Some combinations include:

and **those**	she **says**
as **she**	to **Rome**
by **luck**	we **know**

DACTYLIC: stressed-unstressed-unstressed.

    Some combinations include:

march in.to
un.der the
where in the
beaut.y is

ANAPESTIC: unstressed-unstressed-stressed.

    Some combinations include:

a.la **mode**	in.to **Rome**
in Ja.**pan**	to os.**tend**

Examples are matched using one syllable and some two syllable words to produce various stress patterns. Finding or producing a given stress pattern with one syllable words is more difficult than stress in a single word as with the previous examples.

EXAMPLES:

The following verses illustrate each of the four types of meter. Bold type is used to help you see which syllable is stressed. Syllables are separated by dots. Feet are separated by vertical lines.

TROCHAIC: stressed-unstressed.

    Pan.sies, | **lil**.ies, | **king**.cups, | **dais**.ies.

    Remember: Consonant (T)—stress first—T for two syllables.

IAMBIC: unstressed-stressed.

    A.**long**, | a.**lone**, | a.**las** | he **sat**.

    Remember: Vowel (I)—stress last—I for one unstressed syllable.

DACTYLIC: stressed-unstressed-unstressed.

    Moth.er.ly, | **fath**.er.ly, | **sis**.ter.ly, | **broth**.er.ly.

    Remember: Consonant (D)—stress first.

ANAPESTIC: unstressed-unstressed-stressed.

    As he **spoke**, | in.di.**rect** | in.dis.**creet**, | im.ma.**ture**

    Remember: Vowel (A)—stress last.

Verses are matched on number of feet, and the fact that each foot is one word, except for the last foot in the iambic example and the first foot in the anapestic example. The notes provide mnemonic help in associating critical attributes with the names.

EXAMPLES:

The following verses illustrate each of the four types of meter. Bold type is used to help you see which syllable is stressed. Syllables are separated by dots. Feet are separated by vertical lines.

TROCHAIC: stressed-unstressed.

> **Out** of | **friend**.ship | **came** the | **red**.man
>
> **Teach**.ing | **set**.tlers | **where** the | **deer** ran.
>   (Longfellow)

IAMBIC: unstressed-stressed.

> The **sun** | that **brief** | Dec.**em** | ber **day**
>
> Rose **cheer** | less **ov** | er **hills** | of **gray**.
>   (Whittier)

DACTYLIC: stressed-unstressed-unstressed.

> **Come** to the | **crag** where the | **bea**.con is | **blaz**.ing
>
> **Come** with the | **buck**.ler the | **lance** and the | **bow**.
>   (Scott)

The final foot in each line is incomplete. Don't let this confuse you.

ANAPESTIC: unstressed-unstressed-stressed.

> The **pop** | lars are **felled** | **fare**.well | to the **shade**
>
> And the **whis** | per.ing **sound** | of the **cool** | col.on.**nade**.
>   (Cowper)

In the first line, the first and third feet are incomplete. Don't let this confuse you. Poets often use incomplete feet.

Verses are matched on number of feet and number of lines. Dactylic and anapestic verses include some incomplete feet.

EXAMPLES:

The following stanzas again illustrate the four types of meter.

TROCHAIC: stressed-unstressed:

> As near **│ por.te │ bel.lo │ ly**.ing
> On the │ **gen**.tly │ **swell**.ing │ **flood**,
> At mid │ **night** with │ **stream**.ers │ **fly**.ing
> Our tri │ **umph**.ant │ **na**.vy │ **rode**.

Lines 2 and 4 both end on the stressed syllable.

IAMBIC: unstressed-stressed.

> Good **mor │** row **to │** the **day │** so **fair**,
> Good **mor │** row **sir │** to **you**:
> Good **mor │** row **to │** mine **own │** torn **hair**
> Be.**dab │** bled **with │** the **dew**.
> (Herrick)

Lines 1 and 3 each have four feet where lines 2 and 4 have only 3 feet.

DACTYLIC: stressed-unstressed-unstressed.

> **Moth**.er, dear │ **Moth**.er! the │ **years** have been │ **long**
> **Since** last I │ **list**.ened your │ **lul**.la.by │ **song**;
> **Sing**, then, and │ **un**.to my │ **soul** it shall │ **seem**
> **Wo**.man.hood's │ **years** have been │ **on**.ly a │ **dream**.
> (Allen)

ANAPESTIC: unstressed-unstressed-stressed.

> I am **mon │** arch of **all │ │** I sur.**vey**;
> My **right │** there is **none │** to dis.**pute**:
> From the **cen │** tre all **round │** to the **sea**
> I am **lord │** of the **fowl │** and the **brute**.
> (Cowper)

Line 2 starts with an incomplete foot.

Stanzas have been used rather than just verses. More exceptions have been introduced. The iambic stanza also indicates that different lines may have differing numbers of feet.

EXAMPLES:

Many poets use mixed meter to produce a particular effect. That is, one line will use one meter while the next will shift to another meter. OR they may shift meter within a given line. For each of the following stanzas the meter is indicated.

> If the **heart** | of **man** | is de.**pressed** | with **cares,**
> The **mist** | is dis.**pelled** | when a **wo** | man ap.**pears.**
> (Gay)

This stanza is primarily anapestic; however, in line 1 the second and fourth feet are iambic and in line 2 the first foot is iambic.

A common pattern is to alternate iambic and anapestic:

> That the **low** | est **boughs** | and the **brush** | wood **sheaf**
> Round the **elm** | tree **bole** | are in **tin** | y **leaf,**
> While the **chaf** | finch **sings** | on the **orch** | ard **bough**
> In **Eng.land** | —**now!**
> (Browning)

The last foot uses a pause instead of an unstressed syllable.

The following is a blend of dactylic and trochaic:

> **Beau.**ti.ful | **Ev.**e.lyn | **hope** is | **dead.**
> (Browning)

The last foot ends on a stressed syllable, a masculine ending.

As the variations become extreme the poetry tends toward free verse. Frost here uses iambic and anapestic.

> Two **roads** | di.**verged** | in a **yel** | low **wood,**
> And **sor** | ry I **could** | not **trav** | el **both**
> And **be** | one **trav** | eller, **long** | I **stood**
> And **looked** | down **one** | as **far** | I **could**
> To **where** | it **bent** | in the **und** | er **growth.**
> (Frost)

Note to Sample Lesson

These special cases are introduced at the end of the example presentation to indicate to the student some of the difficult cases he/she may encounter.

PRACTICE:

For each of the following words or phrases check the column which corresponds to the type of meter involved.

trochaic	iambic	dactylic	anapestic	other	
□	□	□	□	□	return
□	□	□	□	□	syllable
□	□	□	□	□	maintain
□	□	□	□	□	beneath
□	□	□	□	□	yesterday
□	□	□	□	□	summer
□	□	□	□	□	habituate
□	□	□	□	□	reproduce
□	□	□	□	□	gallantly
□	□	□	□	□	whatsoever
□	□	□	□	□	represent
□	□	□	□	□	introduce
□	□	□	□	□	resurrection
□	□	□	□	□	convince
□	□	□	□	□	superintendence
□	□	□	□	□	irreligious
□	□	□	□	□	directorate

FEEDBACK:

The correct classification is indicated below—stressed syllables are indicated by bold type.

trochaic	iambic	dactylic	anapestic	other		
☐	☑	☐	☐	☐	re **turn**	
☐	☐	☑	☐	☐	**syl** la ble	
☐	☐	☐	☐	☑	**main tain**	
☐	☑	☐	☐	☐	be **neath**	
☐	☐	☑	☐	☐	**yes** ter day	
☑	☐	☐	☐	☐	**sum** mer	
☐	☑	☐	☐	☐	ha **bit** | u **ate**	Did 2 feet in the word fool you?
☐	☐	☐	☑	☐	re pro **duce**	
☐	☐	☑	☐	☐	**gal** lant ly	
☑	☐	☐	☐	☐	**what** so | **ev** er	Did a compound word (2 feet) fool you?
☐	☐	☐	☑	☐	re pre **sent**	
☐	☐	☐	☑	☐	in tro **duce**	
☑	☐	☐	☐	☐	**res** ur | **rec** tion	2 feet again
☐	☐	☐	☐	☑	**con vince**	
☐	☐	☑	☐	☐	su per in | **tend** ence	Lacks an additional unstressed syllable
☑	☐	☐	☐	☐	**ir** re | li gious	
☐	☑	☐	☐	☐	di **rec** | to **rate**	

PRACTICE:

For each of the following stanzas check the column which corresponds to the type of meter involved.

	trochaic	iambic	dactylic	anapestic	other

1.☐ ☐ ☐ ☐ ☐   Out of the dusk and the glittering
Splendor of stars and of nebulae,
Out of the night with its magical
Breath of the wind from the galaxy.
                 (Wood)

2.☐ ☐ ☐ ☐ ☐   Thus I
Pass by,
And die
As one
Unknown
And gone.
         (Herrick)

3.☐ ☐ ☐ ☐ ☐   When I consider how my light is spent,
Ere half my days, in this dark world and wide. . .
             (Milton)

4.☐ ☐ ☐ ☐ ☐   Cannon to right of them,
Cannon to left of them,
Cannon in front of them
Volleyed and thundered.
             (Tennyson)

FEEDBACK:

The correct classification is indicated below—stressed syllables are indicated by bold type.

trochaic · iambic · dactylic · anapestic · other

1. ☐ ☐ ☑ ☐ ☐
Out of the | **dusk** and the | **glit**.ter.ing
Splend.or of | **stars** and of | **neb**.u.lae,
Out of the | **night** with its | **mag**.i.cal
Breath of the | **wind** from the | **gal**.ax.y.
        (Wood)

2. ☐ ☑ ☐ ☐ ☐
Thus **I**
Pass **by**
And **die**
As **one**
Un.**known**
And **gone.**
     (Herrick)

3. ☐ ☑ ☐ ☐ ☐
When **I** | con.**sid** | er **how** | my **light** | is **spent**
Ere **half** | my **days,** | in **this** | dark **world** | and **wide**. . .
        (Milton)

4. ☐ ☐ ☑ ☐ ☐
Can.non to | **right** of them,
Can.non to | **left** of them,
Can.non in | **front** of them
Vol.leyed and | **thun**.dered.
        (Tennyson)

The last foot is missing one unstressed syllable. This is a common practice as we have seen. Don't let incomplete-ending feet confuse you.

PRACTICE:

For each of the following stanzas check the column which corresponds to the
type of meter involved.

trochaic
iambic
dactylic
anapestic
other

5.☐ ☐ ☐ ☐ ☐   I arise from dreams of thee
                In the first sweet sleep on night.
                            (Shelly)

6.☐ ☐ ☐ ☐ ☐   Hope is banished,
                Joys are vanished.
                            (Dryden)

7.☐ ☐ ☐ ☐ ☐   When the end of the day is at hand,
                And the cattle are penned for the night,
                When the darkness possesses the land,
                And the lamp with its wavery light,
                Is a beacon to summon us home
                From the hill or the vale or the foam,. . .
                            (Anon)

8.☐ ☐ ☐ ☐ ☐   Now the day is over
                Night is drawing nigh;
                Shadows of the evening
                Steal across the sky.
                            (Gould)

FEEDBACK:

The correct classification is indicated below—stressed syllables are indicated by bold type.

	trochaic	iambic	dactylic	anapestic	other

5.☑ ☐ ☐ ☐ ☐   **I** a **|** **rise** from **|** **dreams** of **|** **thee**
In the **|** **first** sweet **|** **sleep** of **|** **night.**
                 (Shelley)

                 Both lines use masculine endings (i.e., they end in stressed syllables causing an incomplete foot).

6.☑ ☐ ☐ ☐ ☐   **Hope** is **|** **banish**.ed,
Joys are **|** **vanish**.ed,
                     (Dryden)

7.☐ ☐ ☐ ☑ ☐   When the **end** **|** of the **day** **|** is at **hand,**
And the **cat** **|** tle are **penned** **|** for the **night**
When the **dark** **|** ness pos.**ses** **|** es the **land,**
And the **lamp** **|** with its **wav** **|** er.y **light,**
Is a **bea** **|** con to **sum** **|** mon us **home**
From the **hill** **|** or the **vale** **|** or the **foam,** . . .
                 (Anon)

                 Trouble may have been words split between feet. This is often necessary to attain a given meter pattern.

8.☑ ☐ ☐ ☐ ☐   **Now** the **|** **day** is **|** **ov**.er
Night is **|** **draw**.ing **|** **nigh;**
Shad.ows **|** of the **|** **even**.ing
Steal a **|** **cross** the **|** **sky.**
                 (Gould)

                 Lines 2 and 4 end on stressed syllables and have incomplete feet. This should not confuse you by now.

PRACTICE:

For each of the following stanzas check the column which corresponds to the type of meter involved.

9.☐ ☐ ☐ ☐ ☐   The poplars are felled farewell to the shade
                           And the whispering sound of the cool colonnade
                           The winds play no longer and sing on the leaves
                           Nor Ouse on his bosom their image receives.
                                     (Cowper)

10.☐ ☐ ☐ ☐ ☐   The monarch saw and shook
                               And bade no more rejoice;
                           All bloodless waxed his look,
                               And tremulous his voice.
                                 (Byron)

11.☐ ☐ ☐ ☐ ☐   Something there is that doesn't love a wall
                               That sends the frozen-ground-swell under it. . .
                                   (Frost)

12.☐ ☐ ☐ ☐ ☐   My heart rebels against my generation
                               That talks of freedom and is slave to riches. . .
                                 (Santayana)

FEEDBACK:

The correct classification is indicated below—stressed syllables are indicated by bold type.

| | trochaic | iambic | dactylic | anapestic | other |

9.☐ ☐ ☐ ☑ ☐   The **pop** | lars are **felled** | **fare**.well | to the **shade**
And the **whis** | per.ing **sound** | of the **cool** | col.on.**nade**
The **winds** | play no **lon** | ger and **sing** | in the **leaves**
Nor **Ouse** | of his **bos** | om their **im** | age re.**ceives**.
(Cowper)

This one is difficult. Lines 2, 3, and 4 each leave off the first unstressed syllable. Also the third foot in line one is iambic. Do you see how this is basically anapestic with some iambic substitutions.

10.☐ ☑ ☐ ☐ ☐   The **mon** | arch **saw** | and **shook**
And **bade** | no **more** | re.**joice**;
All **blood** | less **waxed** | his **look**,
And **trem** | u.lous | his **voice**.
(Byron)

11.☑ ☐ ☐ ☐ ☐   **Some**.thing | **there** is | **that** doesn't | **love** a | **wall**,
That | **sends** the | **fro**.zen- | **ground**-swell | **un**.der | it. . .
(Frost)

This stanza has 2 difficult spots. Treating the word "doesn't" as a single unstressed syllable is forced. Also the unstressed syllable for the last foot in line 1 is used as a "pick up" on the second line. The stanza ends with an incomplete foot—on the stressed syllable.

12.☐ ☑ ☐ ☐ ☐   My **heart** | re.**bels** | a.**gainst** | my **gen** | er.a | tion
That **talks** | of **free** | dom and | is **slave** | to **rich** | es. . .
(Santayana)

The last foot in each line ends on an unstressed syllable—similar to ending on a stressed syllable.

PRACTICE:

For each of the following stanzas check the column which corresponds to the type of meter involved.

13.□ □ □ □   As a sloop with a sweep of inacculate wing
              on her delicate spine
        And a keel as steel as a root that holds
              in the sea as she leans.
                  (Shapiro)

14.□ □ □ □   I went to the garden of love
        And I saw what I never had seen,
        A chapel was built in the midst,
        Where I used to play on the green.
                  (Blake)

15.□ □ □ □   Just for a handful of silver he left us,
        Just for a riband to stick in his ceat.
                  (Browning)

16.□ □ □ □   One more unfortunate
        Weary of breath
        Rashly importunate,
        Gone to her death!
        Take her up Tenderly,
        Lift her with care;
        Fashion'd so slenderly,
        Young, and so fair!
                      (Hood)

FEEDBACK:

The correct classification is indicated below—stressed syllables are indicated by bold type.

	trochaic	iambic	dactylic	anapestic	other

13.☐ ☐ ☐ ☑ ☐   As a **sloop** | with a **sweep** | of in.ac | cu.late **wing**
            on her **del** | i.cate **spine**
          And a **keel** | as **steel** | as a **root** | that **holds**
            in the **sea** | as she **leans.**
                  (Shapiro)

This is a very long line for anapestic meter—6 feet per line. Note feet 2 and 4 in the second line both use iambic. Did this confuse you?

14.☐ ☐ ☐ ☑ ☐   I **went** | to the **gar** | den of **love**
          And I **saw** | what I **nev** | er had **seen,**
          A **chap** | el was **built** | in the **midst,**
          Where I | used to **play** | on the **green.**
                  (Blake)

The first, third, and fourth lines begin with an iambic foot or an incomplete anapestic foot. Did this confuse you?

15.☐ ☐ ☑ ☐ ☐   **Just** for a | **hand.**ful of | **sil.**ver he | **left** us,
          Just for a | **rib.**and to | **stick** in his | **ceat.**
                  (Browning)

The first line ends with an incomplete dactylic foot. The last unstressed syllable is missing. The second line has only one stressed syllable in the last foot. This is a masculine ending for a dactylic meter.

FEEDBACK:

The correct classification is indicated below—stressed syllables are indicated by bold type.

	trochaic	iambic	dactylic	anapestic	other	
16.	☐	☐	☑	☐	☐	**One** more un | **fort**.un.ate **Wear**.y of | **breath** **Rash**.ly im | **port**.un.ate, **Gone** to her | **death!** **Take** her up | **tend**.er.ly, **Lift** her with | **care;** **Fash**.ion'd so | **slen**.der.ly, **Young,** and so | **fair!** (Hood)

> Note: Lines 2, 4, 6, and 8 all end with a single stressed syllable. This is a masculine ending for dactylic meter. Don't let such endings confuse you.

This concludes the sample lesson on poetic meters. A test has not been included. It would be very similar to the practice except feedback would be omitted or included only at the end after the student had responded and turned in his/her paper.

SUMMARY	*TEACHING COORDINATE CONCEPTS*
COORDINATE CONCEPTS	*1. A concept taxonomy is a diagram which is constructed to indicate subordinate, superordinate, and co-ordinate relationships between a set of related concepts. When a super-ordinate concept is divided into subordinate concepts, the subordi-*

nate concepts for a single superordinate concept are called coordinate concepts.

CONCEPT ATTRIBUTES

2. *Critical attributes are those characteristics which are used to discriminate instances of coordinate concepts from one another. Necessary attributes are those characteristics that characterize members of the superordinate concept and are hence necessary for identification but which do not discriminate instances of coordinate concepts from one another. Variable attributes are the critical attributes of a set of coordinate concepts which are subordinate to the concept being taught by a given lesson.*

CONCEPT DEFINITION

3. *A concept definition identifies the superordinate concept, and states the critical attributes and how these attributes are combined in order to define the coordinate concept classes.*

INSTANCE SELECTION RULE

4. *Instances should be selected so that the variable attribute possibilities are adequately represented. Nonexamples should be selected from among the examples of coordinate concept classes (close-in nonexamples). Some nonexamples*

should be selected from the examples of coordinate concepts
once removed (far-out nonexamples).

**DIAGNOSTIC
TEST**

5. *Diagnostic test for coordinate concepts. 1. Select approximately
equal numbers of easy and hard
examples from each of the coordinate concept classes. 2. Select several far-out nonexamples from coordinate concepts once removed. 3.
The instances should be arranged in
random order using either a short
answer or matching format.*

**SCORING A
DIAGNOSTIC
TEST**

6. *Scoring a diagnostic test for coordinate concepts.*

   a. *A correct classification score
   for each coordinate concept is
   the number of examples of
   that concept correctly classified. The total correct classification score is the sum of the
   correct classification scores for
   each coordinate concept plus
   the number of far-out nonexamples correctly classified.*

   b. *Errors can be sorted into
   N(N-1) specific classification
   errors (where N is the number
   of coordinate concept classes).*

   c. *Undergeneralization on concept A occurs when examples
   are classified as examples of
   concept B, C, etc.*

    d. *Overgeneralization on concept A occurs when examples of concepts B, C, etc. are classified as examples of concept A, etc.*

    e. *Misconception occurs whenever a student makes both under- and overgeneralization errors as a result of considering one or more variable attributes critical.*

PRESENTATION FORM SEQUENCE RULE

7. *Presentation form sequence rule for coordinate concepts. When a set of coordinate concepts is being taught, use the following sequence: $rule_1 \rightarrow rule_2 \rightarrow rule_3 \rightarrow example_1 \rightarrow example_2 \rightarrow example_3 \rightarrow practice_1 \rightarrow practice_2 \rightarrow practice_3$ where the "example" and "practice" presentations are repeated as necessary to provide attribute matching and divergence.*

ATTRIBUTE MATCHING RULE

8. *Attribute matching rule for coordinate concepts. In "example" presentations use a series of divergent matched-example sets. In "practice" presentations use a divergent set of examples from the various coordinate concepts, randomly sequenced to avoid undesirable prompts.*

ATTRIBUTE ISOLATION RULE

9. *Attribute isolation rule for coordinate concepts. In "example" presentations use attention focusing devices to direct the student's attention to how the values of the critical attributes change from one coordinate concept to the other.*

INSTANCE DIFFICULTY RULE

10. *Instance difficulty rule for coordinate concepts. Use an easy-to-hard sequence on "example" presentations and a random sequence on "practice" presentations.*

CHAPTER 11
STEP 8:
FORMATIVE AND SUMMATIVE EVALUATION

The final step in the design of concept instruction includes procedures for evaluating the effectiveness of the instructional materials in order to provide data for refinement of the instruction. The data collected for this evaluation include qualitative as well as quantitative information.

Evaluation of instructional materials involves four basic processes. The first three are "formative" procedures in which the instructional materials are evaluated at various points during the development. The fourth part is "summative" evaluation, designed to determine the extent to which the materials adequately enable the student to effectively and efficiently classify newly encountered instances of concepts being taught.

The four steps in the evaluation of your instructional materials and tests include:

1. A review and critique of the content by subject matter consultants.
2. A tryout of the instructional materials on a one-to-one basis.
3. A tryout of the instructional materials with a group of students.
4. A tryout of the instructional materials in the actual learning environment.

**CONTENT
REVIEW**

Prior to formal instructional development, other subject matter consultants should review and critique the definitions and instances. Following instructional development, they should review the content of the completed materials.

The first part of the instructional materials evaluation process is more qualitative than quantitative. Most concepts are determined by consensus. Having other subject matter consultants review the content can help assure that the definitions and instances used reflect this consensus. Because of their naivety, students often contribute little to this part of the evaluation.

Concept definitions should be reviewed before all of the instances are selected. Should modifications be suggested in the inclusion and/or relationship of the critical attributes, these changes can then be reflected in the instances selected. When your consultants disagree, each should prepare a brief note indicating the rationale for including, excluding, or changing the specified relationship between attributes. This documentation will assist you in a final arbitration of the differences and in justifying your final choice of a definition.

Following their selection the instances should also be reviewed by your consultants. This can be done in part by asking your consultants to classify the instances. The classifications by the consultants should agree with your own classifications of the instances. In some content areas there will be certain instances on which the consultants will not agree. When such disagreement occurs, the representation of the critical attributes should be identified for the controversial instance(s), and the reason(s) why the instance(s) is an example or nonexample should be specified in writing. These controversial instances are often valuable to teach fine discriminations. For these controversial instances the "attribute help" material (Chapter 7, Step 6) is especially valuable. The justifications by your consultants will be useful in preparing this help. Instances on which a majority of the reviewers cannot agree should be dropped from the instruction and tests.

Both the definition and instance review procedures can and should be accomplished prior to developing the instructional materials. When the instructional development has been completed, the materials should again be reviewed and critiqued. The emphasis should be on the content, but the consultants may also be invited to comment on the instructional design. Such comments usually include editorial remarks and suggestions on directions for implementation of the instructional materials.

ONE-TO-ONE TRYOUT   *While you observe, have one student work through the materials in order to evaluate the clarity of the directions and of the various content components.*

The second part of the formative evaluation is a tryout of the instruction with a student. While the student works through the instruction you observe and take notes. The purpose of this one-to-one tryout is to identify editorial problems, to reveal any misunderstandings of the directions, and to point out those definitions, instances, or instructional aids which are unclear.

When conducting a one-to-one evaluation the following guidelines may be helpful:

1. Encourage the student to make written comments directly on the instructional materials.
2. Encourage the student to be critical, not just complimentary.
3. Work with the student to clarify segments of the instruction which are not clear.
4. Keep notes on student comments as well as your own observations.

5.   Ask the student to indicate confidence in his/her answers on practice and test displays.

A confidence rating can be obtained by a scale and directions similar to the following. The student is asked to mark the appropriate response on each practice and test item.

A.   Sure   *If you think that your chances of being right are very good.*

B.   Unsure   *If you think that your chances of being right are just about 50:50 (for example, if you can't decide between two answers).*

C.   Guess   *If you think that your chances of being right are not too good.*

Confidence data are useful in estimating retention of concepts learned. If a student has a good score and a high confidence rating, then it is likely that he/she will remember the content; a good score and a low confidence rating is an indication that the student understood the content for the test but will likely not retain the content over time. A good score and a low confidence rating is also an indication that the instruction was inadequate. A low score and high confidence would indicate a faulty test key, too much prompting in the instruction, or poor student motivation or attitude.

When you have completed the one-to-one tryout, study the data for possible revisions of the instruction. If numerous changes are required, conduct a second one-to-one tryout after revisions have been made. All major revisions of the instructional materials should be completed before the third part of the formative evaluation process.

GROUP TRYOUT   *Conducting an evaluation of the instructional materials by using a group of students will provide information on error patterns to diagnose potential difficulties in the instructional materials.*

The final step in formative evaluation involves a group tryout of the instructional materials. The purpose for evaluating the performance of a group of students is to obtain information on the possibility that classification behavior errors might still be occurring. The instructional materials should be presented to students representing the target population. At least 15 students are required to see if any classification error trends are identifiable. Hopefully, by following the design procedures given in this instructional design guide only minor classification problems will occur. You may check for classification error difficulties by comparing student responses on the pretest/posttest and by use of the diagnostic posttest. Guidelines include the following:

1. For this type of evaluation the pretest and posttest should include the same items. However, remember that the instances used for instruction should not be the same as those used for the tests. Comparing the pretest/posttest performance on individual test items provides data for .possible modifications of the instruction. These paired item responses on the pretest/posttest can be evaluated as follows: (Note: Correct responses are indicated by a "+" and incorrect by a "-".)

> *Pretest - Posttest +.* No problem here, items which show incorrect responses on the pretest and then correct on the posttest demonstrate correct classification learning.

> *Pretest - Posttest -.* When a test item is incorrectly classified on both tests, you can assume that the student has not completely learned the critical attributes. We suggest that more examples demonstrating the variable attributes represented in the test item be included in the instruction.

> *Pretest + Posttest -.* If a test item is correctly answered on the pretest and then incorrectly answered on the posttest, check the correct classification of the item. If correct, it might be that the instruction failed to match or be divergent on certain variable attributes; hence the instruction probably promoted a misconception. You should compare the variable attributes of the test item with those of the instructional instances. Check first the

divergence and matching of instances with those variable attributes to see how the attributes are represented. Adjust where necessary. Also, you might consider some form of attribute isolation help (Chapter 7, Step 6). Variable attributes that can cause misconceptions are often not identified until after the student has taken a posttest.

Pretest + Posttest +. In situations where the items are correctly answered on both tests, it is possible that the test item was over-prompted. Or, perhaps the students knew the concept and thus the concept instruction could be shortened or presented earlier in the curriculum.

2. The diagnostic posttest can also be used for evaluating the instructional materials. The procedures for developing and analyzing a diagnostic posttest are given in Chapter 6, Step 5. You should evaluate individual scoring patterns as well as overall group scoring patterns. The latter evaluation will indicate the total effectiveness of the instruction. That is, the group mean might indicate correct classification, but it might still be possible that the instruction promoted an overgeneralization, undergeneralization, or misconception. If one of these three errors is indicated by the group data, then you have a good idea of how to revise the instruction. On the other hand, individual error patterns might suggest a need for additional review or remedial material for individual students. For each of the three error patterns the following revisions procedures are suggested.

Overgeneralization. This is a discrimination error. The matched instance pairs (example and nonexample) should be checked. Increasing the number of the pairs should correct the problem. The attribute help material should also be checked to see if it adequately focuses attention to the critical attributes.

Undergeneralization. This error occurs when the students fail to generalize. It is indicative of too few difficult instances and insufficient different examples showing the range of the variable attributes. Additional difficult examples should be added. The inclusion of common variable attributes should be checked to see if the range of the concept(s) is being adequately represented.

Misconception. This error problem can be the most difficult to analyze. Usually, some variable attribute that is common to two or more concepts is learned as being critical to a given concept when in fact it is not. To determine which variable attributes are causing the misconception, analyze the examples and nonexamples which were incorrectly classified. The nonexamples classified as examples should be examined in relationship to examples classified as nonexamples to see if there are variable attributes in common. If so, include examples and nonexamples which do not have this variable attribute. Use matching and attribute isolation to focus the students attention on the absence of this variable attribute.

The data collected from the review and two tryouts discussed above should provide useful information for refining the instruction. The learning materials are complete at this stage. The final step in evaluation is to determine if the learning materials meet the goals of the instruction.

LEARNING ENVIRONMENT TRYOUT

Summative evaluation occurs in the actual learning environment for the purpose of determining if the students learn effectively and efficiently from the instruction.

The summative evaluation phase takes place in the setting where the instruction is to be normally used. Its purpose is to determine to what degree the instructional materials meet the goals and objectives of the course of study; that is, can the students when finished with the instruction correctly identify newly encountered instances of the concept(s) taught? Summative evaluation can perform two different functions. First, it can be used for evaluating the instructional objective. Second, it can be used to evaluate possible alternative forms of the instruction. We have emphasized throughout this guide that you should explore alternative designs. A summative evaluation allows you to test these alternatives.

Guidelines for the summative evaluation include the following:

1. The main consideration in conducting a summative evaluation is to tryout the instructional materials in the student's normal learning environment. Students should be directed that the instructional materials are part of their usual learning experiences. Unusual preparations or announcements should be minimized because student reactions to experimental learning situations can influence their usual behavior.

2. The most important evaluation question at this point of development is, ". . .do the instructional materials teach?" The only way to adequately test this question is to compare performance of students who have taken the instruction with those who have not. Randomly assign students from the target population to two groups. One group is given the pretest, instruction, and posttest. The second group is given only the pretest and posttest. This experimental design is summarized as follows:

> *Group 1. Pretest → Instructional Materials → Posttest.*
> *Group 2. Pretest → No Instructional Materials → Posttest.*

For this evaluation the group means (average scores of the students in each group) are compared rather than individual scores or error patterns as in the formative evaluation. There should be no "significant differences" between the two groups on the pretest. But the instructional materials group should have a significantly higher score on the posttest.*

---

*Consult with a statistician for the procedures necessary to determine if the differences you observe are greater than would occur by chance. A description of such statistical procedures is beyond the scope of this book.

3. As mentioned earlier, alternative instructional designs can also be tested with a group comparison design. Test the two different forms of the instruction in the same manner as described above. The two experimental designs would be:

Group 1. Pretest → Instructional Materials A → Posttest.
Group 2. Pretest → Instructional Materials B → Posttest.

One group must have a "significantly" higher score to be able to say one instructional design is better than the other. It is possible to test more than two alternatives simultaneously. Consult with a statistician for the statistical procedures required.

4. To evaluate the efficiency of the instructional materials, time expended in learning the concept(s) should also be collected. Time data should include time used on directions; time needed for testing (both pretest and posttest); time spent on the different learning units of the instruction; and total time. Students can keep good records of their learning time if proper directions are given at the start of instruction. Efficiency can be measured by the same group comparison design described above for determining instructional effectiveness. Comparisons should be made between the groups on time within the program, time on the posttest, and total time. The most efficient design is indicated by the group which requires significantly less time while simultaneously making the same or fewer errors then the comparison group.

SUMMARY STEP 8:

EVALUATION

FORMATIVE AND SUMMATIVE EVALUATION

Evaluation of instructional materials involves both FORMATIVE procedures, evaluation of the materials during development, and SUMMATIVE procedures, evaluation which determines the effec-

tiveness and efficiency of the completed instruction.

The four steps of formative and summative evaluation include:

CONTENT REVIEW

1. *A content review of the instructional materials by subject matter consultants.*

ONE-TO-ONE TRYOUT

2. *A one-to-one tryout of the instructional materials between yourself and a student representative of the target population.*

GROUP TRYOUT

3. *A group tryout of the instructional materials with students from the target population.*

LEARNING ENVIRONMENT TRYOUT

4. *A learning environment tryout of the instructional materials in the real-world instructional setting.*

CHAPTER 12

PUTTING IT ALL TOGETHER

In this book we have defined a series of instructional variables and a strategy for putting these variables together to teach concepts. In this chapter concept lesson development is summarized with an annotated flowchart that may help you design concept lessons.

The Development Process

1. *Decide if a concept lesson is needed.* Chapter 1 defines concepts and Classification behaviors. Chapter 2 gives guidelines for determining when concept lessons may be required. This book should be used only if your lesson involves concepts.

2. *Define your concept.* Chapter 3 defines critical and variable attributes and explains how they are combined to form definitions.

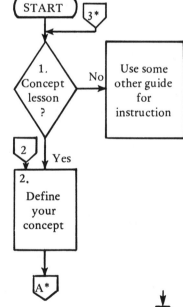

---

*[3] indicates a branch back to this point from later in the flowchart. [3] is used to indicate where the branch originates. [A] means the flowchart is continued on the next page.

195

3. *Collect an instance pool.*
Chapter 4 sets forth the *divergent example rule* and the *matched nonexample rule* which should be considered as you collect instances.

8a. *Content review.*
Chapter 11 indicates that your definition and instances should be reviewed by another content expert. If your consultant finds problems, you should review either the definition and collect more instances, or revise your instances. Have another content review after you have made your revisions.

4. *Estimate difficulty for each instance.* Chapter 5 describes an empirical procedure for determining instance difficulty. If your analysis shows an insufficient difficulty range, you should gather more instances. Be sure your new instances are also reviewed by your subject matter consultant.

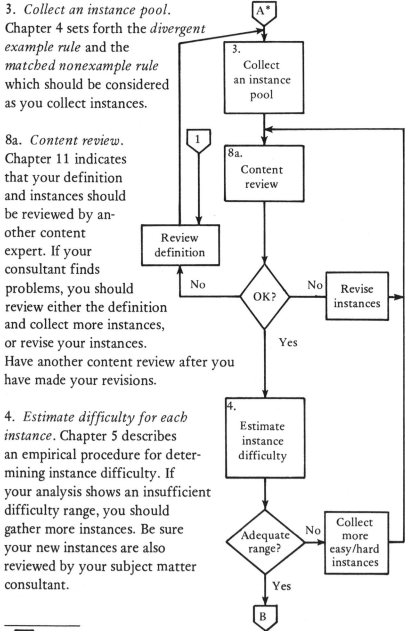

* [A] means the flowchart is continued from the previous page.

5. *Prepare a diagnostic test.* Chapter 6 defines *correct classification* and classification errors. Procedures for selecting instances, writing test items, and scoring the test are described.

6. *Prepare attribute isolation.* Chapter 3 describes attention focusing devices that should accompany the instances.

7. *Design an instructional strategy.* Chapter 8 defines the four primary presentation forms: *rule, example, practice,* and *recall.* Chapter 9 defines an instructional strategy that incorporates the *presentation form sequence rule*, the *attribute isolation rule*, the *attribute matching rule*, and the *instance difficulty rule.* Chapter 10 modifies these rules for teaching *coordinate concepts.*

8b. *One-to-one tryout.* Chapter 11 describes techniques for evaluating your lesson with one or two individual students. After each tryout, materials should be revised and tried with another student until the student-detected difficulties have all been revised.

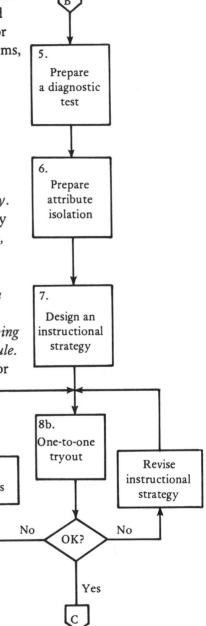

8c. *Group tryout.* Chapter 11 describes two types of analysis for group tryout data—pre/post test analysis and specific classification error analysis. Specific modifications are recommended for various errors which may be detected.

8d. *Learning environment tryout.* Chapter 11 describes procedure and analysis for a complete tryout. If all previous steps have been followed, there should be significant pre/post test gain. If there is insufficient gain, E (see following page) perhaps better examples or a restated definition would improve performance. Make these revisions and compare the two strategies. If there is no gain, D (see following page) the problem is more serious. If everyone passed the pretest, the students probably already know the concept and the lesson should be dropped. If both the pre- and posttest are failed, separate lessons for the critical attributes may need to be added or the lesson may be presented later in the sequence.

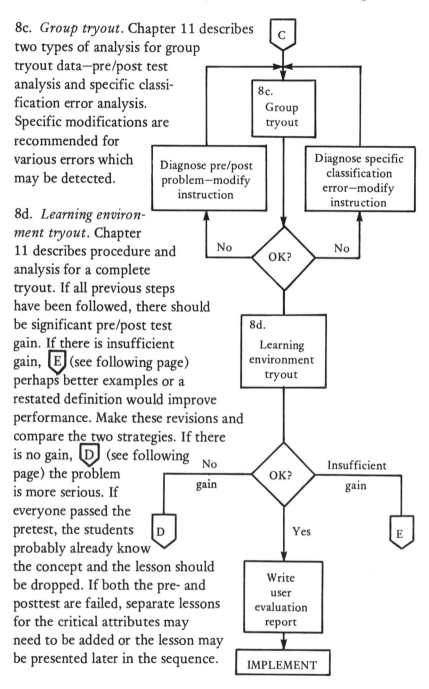

8d. (cont.) *Learning environment tryout.*

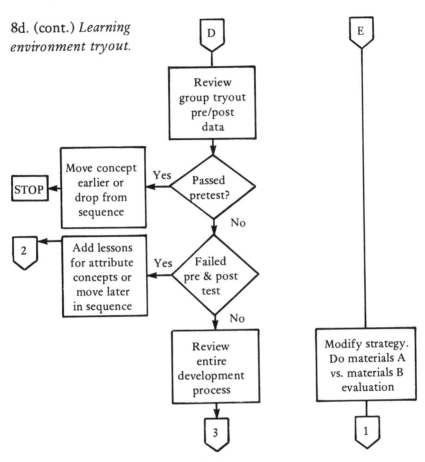

Concept Lessons in the Real World

"I used your procedure but no one can possibly use such a detailed procedure for a whole curriculum in ordinary teaching situations."

This is not an unusual comment for those who have worked their way through *Teaching Concepts* for the first time. How can the detailed design procedures described in this book be used in ordinary classroom situations, where time is at a premium? Perhaps the following recommendations will help.

Start with the tests. Chances are that students are already learning many of the concepts you teach from existing text materials or from classroom presentations, but your tests may not adequately measure concept acquisition.

Identify those concepts in your course that are candidates for concept lessons. Choose the two or three most important concepts and examine the tests that you use to determine whether students have acquired these concepts. Using the guidelines provided in Chapter 5, redesign the tests so that you can diagnose any difficulties students may be having in acquiring these concepts.

Conduct a group tryout. The new tests, your existing instructional procedures, and the group tryout procedures described in Chapter 11 will help you determine the extent to which students are acquiring these two or three important concepts.

Design lessons for problem concepts. If your group tryout shows that there are difficulties, design more effective concept lessons for those concepts and insert them into your regular curriculum. Re-evaluate the next term or year to be sure that the new lesson is doing the job better.

Use an evaluation procedure. When you have designed lessons for the most important concepts, repeat the procedure for those concepts second in importance. Over a period of time you will have evolved significant improvements in your course instruction.

This instructional design guide deals only with teaching concepts. The procedures described have been validated in carefully controlled research studies and, if carefully followed, should result in significantly improved concept acquisition. The authors think that you will find that as you improve the concept instruction in your course, many of the other outcomes you desire will also be improved. All complex rule-using and problem-solving behaviors use concepts as building blocks. If the students really understand the concepts involved, they will find it easier to use these concepts to solve problems.

RESEARCH SUMMARY

The prescriptions for teaching concepts found in this book are not "blue sky" ideas but rather represent the result of careful research studies on concept instruction. The authors have been actively involved in some of this research activity. Some of the most relevant published studies are briefly summarized below.

Proposition No. 1. *Correct classification of newly encountered instances is more probable if during instruction: examples are matched to nonexamples, subsequent examples are divergent from previous examples, and instances range in difficulty from easy to hard.*

This proposition is the basis for the "attribute matching rule" and the "instance difficulty rule" (see chapter 9). The authors have conducted three studies which clearly support this proposition and the design rules which are based on this proposition.

Study 1: Tennyson, R. D., Woolley, F. R., and Merrill, M. D. Exemplar and nonexemplar variables which produce correct concept classification behavior and specified classification errors. *Journal of Educational Psychology,* 1972, *63*, 144-152.

Task. Given passages of poetry indicate which ones involve trochaic meter.

Students. Undergraduate Brigham Young University students.

Treatments. Each treatment consisted of an expository presentation of a definition and 16 instances (eight examples and eight nonexamples).

In treatment *C*, designed to promote correct classification, each example was matched to a nonexample, each subsequent example was divergent from the previous example, and the first four instances were easy (empirically determined as explained in Chapter 5), the next eight medium, and the last four difficult.

In treatment *U*, designed to promote undergeneralization, each example was matched to a nonexample, each subsequent example was divergent from the previous example, but all of the instances were easy.

In treatment *O*, designed to promote overgeneralization, each example was paired with a nonexample but they were not matched, each example was divergent from the previous example, and all of the instances were difficult.

In treatment *M*, designed to promote misconception, each example was paired with a nonexample but they were not matched, the examples were convergent on a single/variable attribute, and the instances ranged from easy to hard as in treatment *C*.

Results. A 30-instance posttest was scored as explained in Chapter 6. As hypothesized, treatment *C* was significantly better than the other groups on the correct classification score. Treatment *U* made significantly more undergeneralization errors than any of the other groups. Treatment *O* made significantly more overgeneralization errors than any of the other groups. Treatment *M* made significantly more misconception errors than any of the other groups.

Study 2: Tennyson, R. D. Effect of negative instances in concept acquisition using a verbal-learning task. *Journal of Educational Psychology*, 1973, *64*, 247-260.

Task. Given sentences with one word modifiers underlined, indicate which are adverbs.

Students. Junior high school students.

Treatments. Experiment one was the same as the Tennyson, Woolley, and Merrill study. Four treatments were used as previously described. Experiment two involved four treatments which were the same as the four treatments already described except that all of the nonexamples were eliminated. That is, treatment *C'* had a divergent set of examples ranging from easy to hard but no nonexamples. Treatment *U'* had a divergent set of easy examples. Treatment *O'* had a divergent set of hard examples. Treatment *M'* had a convergent set of examples which ranged from easy to hard.

Results. A 30-item posttest was scored as explained in Chapter 6. The outcome of experiment one was the same as for Study 1. In experiment two, treatment *C'* made more undergeneralization errors than treatment *C* in experiment 1 in study 2. Treatment *U'* was the same as treatment *U*, more undergeneralization errors. Treatment *O'* was the same as treatment *O*, more overgeneralization errors. Treatment *M'* was the same as treatment *M*, more misconception errors. This study demonstrated that nonexamples are necessary to promote correct classification.

Study 3: Merrill, M. D. and Tennyson, R. D. Concept classification and classification errors as a function of relationship between examples and nonexamples. *Improving Human Performance*, 1977, in press.

Task. Given drawings representing crystal structure indicate which are RX_2 crystals.

Students. Undergraduate Brigham Young University students.

Treatments. The treatments were the same as in study 1 except a control group was added to assess how much was learned.

Results. The same as in study 1. The comparisons with the control group showed that there was learning as a result of the treatment conditions.

Proposition No. 2. *Correct classification of newly encountered instances is more probable if during instruction using "example" presentations each instance is accompanied by attribute isolation and if during instruction using "practice" presentations a learner's response (either right or wrong) is followed by attribute isolation feedback.*

This proposition is the basis for the "attribute isolation rule" (see Chapter 9). The authors and their associates have conducted three studies which clearly support this proposition and the design rule which is based on this proposition.

Study 4: Merrill, M. D. and Tennyson, R. D. Attribute prompting variables in learning classroom concepts. *Instructional Research and Development Working Paper No. 28*, BYU, 1971.

Task. Given passages of poetry indicate which ones involve trochaic meter.

Students. Undergraduate Brigham Young University students.

Treatments. The study involved several treatments but only two are of importance to this proposition. Treatment *C* is exactly the same as treatment *C* in study 1: each example matched to a nonexample, each example divergent from the previous example, and a range of easy to hard instances.

Treatment *C+* is exactly the same as treatment *C* except that attribute isolation which indicated syllables, stress, and poetic feet was added to each of the instances.

Results. A 30-instance posttest was scored for correct classification. There was no attribute isolation on the test items. Treatment *C+* scored significantly higher than did treatment *C*.

Study 5: Young, J. I. The effects of review techniques and instance presentation on concept learning tasks. Unpublished doctoral dissertation, BrighamYoung University, May 1972.

Task. Given passages of poetry indicate which ones involve trochaic meter.

Students. Undergraduate Brigham Young University students.

Treatments. The treatments were the same as *C* and *C+* described for the previous experiments except that the instances were presented in"practice" (inquisitory) rather than "example" (expository) mode.

Results. A 30-instance posttest was scored for correct classification. Treatment *C+* inquisitory scored significantly higher than treatment *C* inquisitory.

Study 6: Tennyson, R. D., Steve, M. W., and Boutwell, R. C. Instance sequence and analysis of instance attribute representation in concept acquisition. *Journal of Educational Psychology*, 1975, *67*, 821-827.

Task. For experiment one, given passages of poetry indicate which ones involve trochaic meter. For experiment two, given drawings representing crystal structure indicate which are RX_2 crystals.

Students. Undergraduate students at Florida State University.

Treatments. There were four treatments in each of the two experiments: treatment *C* was the same as has been previously described. Treatment *C+* was the same as treatment *C+* in study 4. Treatment *C* random was the same instances as in treatment *C* except they were reordered according to a table of random numbers so that the matched and divergent relationships no longer existed. Treatment *C* random + was the same as treatment *C* random with attribute isolation added to each instance. For the meter, attribute isolation indicated stress, syllables, and poetic feet; for the RX_2 crystals, attribute isolation consisted of exploded drawings.

Results. On 30-item posttests for both experiments, treatment *C+* had a significantly higher correct classification score than any other groups. Treatment *C+* random and treatment *C* scored significantly higher than treatment *C* random but not significantly different from each other. This indicates that the "attribute matching rule" and the "attribute isolation rule" are additive, that is, using one or the other will improve performance but using both will improve performance even more.

Our concept research work is continuing. The reader is invited to contribute to this study of the teaching of concepts through his/her own formal or informal research efforts. Our current activities are investigating the teaching of coordinate concepts, the relative contribution of each of the primary presentation forms, and the importance of a rule —►example —►practice sequence. Subsequent editions of this manual will incorporate our findings.

INDEX